GOOD RETURNS

GOOD RETURNS

Making Money
by Morally Responsible Investing

George P. Schwartz, CFA
with William J. Koshelnyk

Foreword by Lou Holtz

Published by The Barnabas Agency and Geodi Publishing

ISBN: 978-0-9844042-0-9

Library of Congress Control Number: 2010922255

Printed in the United States of America by Edwards Brothers, Inc., Ann Arbor,
Michigan

To Judi — my Pearl of Great Value

(Matthew 13:44)

Contents

Acknowledgements

Since my last book, published in 1995, I had forgotten how difficult it is to actually complete a manuscript like this one. More talented and experienced authors, I'm sure, can do it more efficiently; but for me, it was tedious. If not for my collaborator, Bill Koshelnyk, I would never have been able to put it together.

A special thanks to my colleague, co-portfolio manager and son, Tim Schwartz, for suggesting that I write this book. In mid-2008, he said, "A book on Morally Responsible Investing should be written, and no one in the entire world is more qualified than you to write it." With that, and the encouragement of Paul Roney, Chairman of our Catholic Advisory Board, I was psyched to write.

Thanks to my staff, analysts and portfolio managers who had to pick up the slack at the office when I was buried in research for this book. Oddly enough, while I was preoccupied with this project, the investment performance of all our Ave Maria Mutual Funds improved. I'm sure it was just a coincidence.

— George P. Schwartz
  March 2010

Foreword

Good Returns details the methodology used to produce excellent investment results for serious investors who care deeply that none of their money is supporting the greatest evil of our time, abortion. This book delves deeply into Morally Responsible Investing and explains the approach used by the Ave Maria Mutual Funds.

I feel qualified to write this foreword, as I have been on the Ave Maria Board for two years and have observed George Schwartz and his associates up close. They are talented, hardworking, trustworthy good leaders, and their integrity and character are excellent. They have received many awards including the prestigious 2009 Lipper Fund Award for outstanding investment performance of the Ave Maria Growth Fund, which ranked first out of 653 funds in its category (Multi-Cap Core) for the three years ended December 31, 2008.

After Tom Monaghan sold the Detroit Tigers and Domino's Pizza in the '90s, he and his long-time friend, Bowie Kuhn, dedicated themselves to Catholic causes. In 2001, with the help of their friend, George P. Schwartz, the three of them started the Ave Maria Mutual Funds. George, a life-long Catholic (and a big Notre Dame fan) is CEO of Schwartz Investment Counsel, Inc. of Bloomfield Hills, Michigan, a registered investment adviser. His firm has done an outstanding job of prudently managing these pro-life mutual funds.

Good Returns describes how the Funds' professional portfolio managers follow the moral guidelines established by our Catholic Advisory Board. The author lays out in detail the investing principles behind the excellent performance of these unique Funds, and conveys important insights gained through his four decades of managing institutional portfolios. In this easy-to-read book, Schwartz has issued a call to arms for people of faith who want to pursue investment success while trying to make a real difference in society.

This is a serious effort that grows out of a deep moral commitment. And Schwartz and his team bring a great work ethic to it (team work and work ethic are things I know something about). These guys have a sophisticated investment approach, and they are highly focused. They don't spend much time on the golf course — no time for that. In one of my own books, *Wins, Losses, and Lessons,* I wrote, "I would never hire a guy who keeps golf clubs in the trunk of his car." George doesn't — believe me, I've played with him — perhaps that's why the investment performance of the Ave Maria Mutual Funds has been so good.

One of my favorite sayings is, "Nothing on this earth is standing still. It's either growing or it's dying." This book chronicles a movement, a *growing* movement of morally responsible investors. That movement is favorably impacting corporate behavior by encouraging corporate America to modify policies that conflict with traditional moral values, and to adopt policies that show respect for the sanctity of human life.

— Lou Holtz
March 2010

Introduction

Wise investment management of our worldly resources is a moral imperative.

Why? Because prudent investing is essential to meeting future material needs — which is a basic responsibility — to provide for ourselves and not rely on the government to support us. It also makes charity possible, the means by which we put love for others into meaningful and effective action.

You probably have never heard this point proclaimed from the pulpit of any church you've attended, and that's understandable. Other than encouraging congregational giving or the support of some worthy cause, clergy generally don't touch on investment matters in their preaching.

But there is scriptural warrant for managing resources wisely. The Bible is full of admonitions about *counting the cost* and *making right choices*, employing economic metaphors which can be read in a pragmatic as well as a spiritual sense. Moreover, there is a rich Judeo-Christian ethical tradition that has delved into all areas of business conduct and financial concern, from Old Testament times right up to the present. Its most recent expression is the encyclical, *Caritas in Veritate*, in which Pope Benedict XVI explores the linkage between wealth and moral purpose.

Investing is a critical component of financial management. And it is a distinctly moral act, carrying with it the obligations of productivity and the exercise of good judgment — as in Jesus' "Parable of the Talents." You'll recall that in the tale, a rich master, about to depart on a journey, gives each of three servants money (talents) which they are instructed to manage until his return. Two of the servants show a profit, gaining praise for their initiative. But when the third servant merely restores the original amount he had been given, the master is incensed. Why had that servant timidly hidden the money in fear of losing it, when he might have at least deposited it with the bankers?

The parable testifies, both implicitly and explicitly, to the rightness of investing with the intention of making resources grow. It doesn't endorse wild speculation (as it specifically rejects the passive inaction of the timid servant), but it tells us that we are to do the best we can with what the master — God — has given us.

The stock market meltdown of 2008-2009 was a particular affront to those of us who try to approach investing with personal ethics and moral dignity. The economic collapse represented more than a normal cyclical correction. Rather, it resulted from an especially noxious combination of institutional irresponsibility, political influence peddling, and personal venality. We shouldn't be surprised that restoring trust in the system has taken time.

There are lessons to be learned from this great debacle, the foremost of which is the essential role of prudence. It is wise — as indeed, it is morally appropriate — to invest with prudence and caution. When we do so, we have every right to expect a reward for the efforts we have made and the risks we have borne. As the Apostle Paul put it, "...when the plowman plows and the thresher threshes, they ought to do so in the hope of sharing in the harvest."[1]

Such an expectation is light-years away from the so-called "Prosperity Gospel" that has been the staple of tent preachers and tel-evangelists over the years. The essential message of those misbegotten hucksters is: *Send me your money, and God will reward you for your sac-*

---

1   1 Corinthians 9:10.

rifice by making you rich. In contrast, this book is about participating in the capital markets in a purposeful, reasoned and ethical way that can achieve legitimate (religiously endorsed) investment objectives while not entangling you in morally questionable business practices.

What kinds of "morally questionable" practices am I talking about? While my subject isn't business ethics, per se, it goes without saying that I would urge you to resist being drawn into financial dealings that shave the law or raise the ethical concerns brought to light during our recent Wall Street travails (Bernard Madoff's infamous Ponzi scheme comes to mind). More than that, however, my intention is to demonstrate how you can get *good returns* on your investments while avoiding securities of corporations that are engaged in activities contradicting key Christian values — in particular, those that violate certain core teachings of the Catholic Church.

In these pages I will acquaint you with an approach to prudent — and profitable — investing that can help you provide for your future, accumulate reserves for charitable giving, or achieve any number of other morally sound financial objectives. I will show that my methods are based on well established investment practices, argue that they are not only ethically valid, but entirely practical (even financially astute), and cite actual, real-life investing experience to support my assertions.

By what authority do I offer this advice? Let me state at the outset that I do not speak for the Church. While I am a lifelong Catholic, I'm not a priest, theologian or religious scholar. Rather, I'm an investment counselor and mutual fund manager — in fact the co-founder and manager of the largest family of Catholic mutual funds in operation today, the Ave Maria Mutual Funds. My purpose in writing this book is to demonstrate that investors who seek to pursue the goal of financial security in a spirit of moral probity can obtain excellent results in a way that is consistent with their ethical principles and religious beliefs — or, as it might be put, *investing while taking the moral high ground.*

The documented history of the Ave Maria Mutual Funds (all of which screen out shares of companies that support abortion or pornography) demonstrates that one need not sacrifice integrity for the sake of *good returns*. Indeed, we have achieved outstanding investment performance for our 25,000-plus shareholders. Most notable are our three 4-star-rated funds — the Ave Maria Rising Dividend Fund (AVEDX), the Ave Maria Growth Fund (AVEGX) and the Ave Maria Opportunity Fund (AVESX) — as determined by the mutual fund rating service, Morningstar. In addition, the Ave Maria Growth Fund was singled out by the Lipper organization for the 2009 Lipper Fund Award. It was ranked Number 1 out of 653 funds in its category (Multi-Cap Core) for the three-year period ended December 31, 2008.[2]

Such performance during a period all will recognize as difficult (to say the least) is something we are proud of. It gives me a high degree of confidence in the validity of my insights, gained as they are, from practical experience blending investment management with moral conviction.

And so, I will attempt to show you how to *do well* by *doing good.* If you sense that the arguments I put before you are true, then I urge you to consider what they imply for your own investing. Because the moral imperative of wise investment management demands that we conduct our financial lives with the understanding that in all we do, we stand under the watchful eye of God. In the words of Pope Benedict, "every economic decision has a moral consequence."[3]

2   See Appendix C for a description of Morningstar ratings and for information on the performance of the Ave Maria Mutual Funds through December 31, 2009.

3   *Caritas in Veritate*, Section 37.

chapter 1

Money & Morality

It would be downright silly to claim that only good, moral and religious people can succeed at investing. There are numerous examples of dirty rotten scoundrels who have made killings in the stock market. So many, in fact, that the idea of ruthlessness as a prerequisite to investment success is a common cliché — the "Gordon Gekko"[1] model, as it were. Yet, I am convinced that there is a certain relationship between conviction in spiritual matters and acumen in analyzing the market. I think that relationship lies primarily in two areas: (1) an ability to see beyond surface features into inner realities; and (2) a willingness to dedicate oneself to disciplined practices over time.

Both Judaism and Christianity have spoken profusely on economic matters, the "Parable of the Talents" being only one of the more prominent New Testament passages that address the subject.[2] Indeed,

---

1   Referring to Gordon Gekko, a fictional character known for his insistence that "Greed is good!" in the 1987 motion picture, "Wall Street," as portrayed by actor, Michael Douglas. The Gordon Gekko image has proven so durable that a "Wall Street" sequel is in the works.

2   This tale suggests much about financial life in first-century Palestine, since what would have been gained if the fearful servant had deposited his "talent" with the bankers is offered as the minimum option available (of course, Jesus doesn't tell us anything about the master's concern with preserving *principal*).

the Bible is filled with commercial imagery and financial references that have provided the basis for centuries of reflection on economic and business matters. Some of them comment quite explicitly on the virtue of investing for the sake of future security — to wit:

> "A good man leaves an inheritance to his children's children." (Proverbs 13:22)

> "Whoever does not provide for relatives and especially family members has denied the faith and is worse than an unbeliever." (1 Timothy 5:8)

In the Catholic tradition, there has been a remarkable degree of consistency among thinkers who have turned their attention to the concerns of economic life.[3] Among the monumental Catholic pronouncements is Pope Leo XIII's encyclical, *Rerum Novarum*. Issued in 1891, at a time when the ideas of Karl Marx and other revolutionary thinkers were causing socialist ferment in the industrialized nations, *Rerum Novarum* offered a comprehensive Christian vision of the proper relationship between capital and labor, the basic components of economic exchange.

One of the points the encyclical makes most forcefully is its defense of private property as an economic necessity related to our fundamental human nature. Because "man alone among the animal creation is endowed with reason," wrote Leo, "it must be within his right to possess things not merely for temporary and momentary use, as other living things do, but to have and to hold them in stable and permanent possession. . . ."[4] While the Pope was focusing primarily on ownership of tangible property (i.e.: land), rather than corporate shares, he acknowledged the importance of making provision for the future (that is, of *investing*), noting that ownership gives man the

---

3   Just about the only major economic question on which the mind of the Church has undergone a major change is the definition of *usury*. Deemed immoral since Old Testament times, the practice of lending money at interest was theologically acceptable by the Seventeenth Century.

4   *Rerum Novarum*, Paragraph 6.

power "to exercise his choice not only as to matters that regard his present welfare, but also about those which he deems may be for his advantage in time yet to come."[5]

Leo was no *laissez faire* capitalist. He insisted that the interests of society in general, and of the poor in particular, must be adequately addressed for the economic order to be considered properly Christian. "However the earth may be apportioned among private owners," he wrote, "it does not cease to serve the common interests of all."[6]

Forty years later, Leo's successor, Pius XI, strengthened the vital connection between economics and morality in the encyclical, *Quadragesimo Anno* (1931). "Even though economics and moral science employs each its own principles in its own sphere," Pius wrote, "it is, nevertheless, an error to say that the economic and moral orders are so distinct from and alien to each other that the former depends in no way on the latter." Citing the unique human capacity to reason, as did Leo, Pius insisted on moral discernment in temporal affairs, "the individual and social nature of things and of men," as he put it, "the purpose which God ordained for all economic life."[7]

Never one to mince words, Pius directed some barbed comments at the corporate culture that had taken hold of the modern world by the 1930s:

> "The laws passed to promote corporate business, while dividing and limiting the risk of business, have given occasion to the most sordid license. For We observe that consciences are little affected by this reduced obligation of accountability; that furthermore, by hiding under the shelter of a joint name, the worst of injustices and frauds are penetrated; and that, too, directors of business companies, forgetful of their trust, betray the rights of those whose savings they have undertaken to administer."[8]

5   *Rerum Novarum*, Paragraph 7
6   *Rerum Novarum*, Paragraph 8.
7   *Quadragesimo Anno*, Paragraph 42.
8   *Quadragesimo Anno*, Paragraph 132.

The final clause in this quotation is an interesting instance of a Pope specifically expressing concern about the rights of shareholders. It suggests a certain shrewd understanding of corporate management on the part of His late Holiness. In the same document Pius castigates profiteering as well:

> "The easy gains that a market unrestricted by any law opens to everybody attracts large numbers to buying and selling goods, and they, their one aim being to make quick profits with the least expenditure of work, raise or lower prices by their uncontrolled business dealings so rapidly according to their own caprice and greed that they nullify the wisest forecasts of producers."[9]

One wonders if Pius dabbled in the markets himself, because he surely had a keen eye. His observation would be as directly applicable to would-be stock manipulators as to those given to wild speculations in commodities.[10]

One of the clearest statements that economics can't be separated from religiously based moral discernment was made in our own time by the late Pope John Paul II. His encyclical, *Centesimus Annas* (1991), was a sweeping commentary on economics, human liberty and the conditions of life in a world that had just witnessed the crumbling of the Berlin Wall, an accomplishment in which John Paul himself had played a major part (as did Ronald Reagan, our greatest President in my view). While summing up the failure of Communism to deliver on its promise of a better life for the struggling masses, the Pope offered some serious words of caution to the Capitalist West, then basking in its triumph over the Marxists. John Paul the Great charged that when

---

9   *Quadragesimo Anno*, Paragraph 132.

10   It would also apply to some modern-day hedge fund operators who use massive amounts of debt leverage to magnify returns at huge risk. The 1998 collapse of Long Term Capital Management subjected the entire U.S. economy to such systematic risk, mitigated only by the intervention of the Federal Reserve Bank of New York. LTCM's founder, John Meriwether (a former trader of mortgage-backed securities at Solomon Brothers) became notorious for using debt leveraged as much as 300-to-1, when the leverage rate of other hedge funds considered aggressive was a mere 4-to-1.

the market system "denies an autonomous existence and value to morality, law, culture and religion, it agrees with Marxism, in the sense that it totally reduces man to the sphere of economics and the satisfaction of material needs."[11]

Some in the left-leaning media jumped on that line as proof that John Paul was, in his heart, a sort of soft socialist, which was a fanciful idea at best. Actually, the Pope's words were a perfect example of the balance and perceptiveness which Catholic moral philosophy has brought to human experience throughout the centuries.

Investing and Faith

Scripture offers no record of Jesus advising his disciples to "buy low, and sell high," but I believe that religiously based moral discernment enriches investing judgment. Companies that appreciate in value — and whose shares rise correspondingly in price — are generally companies that are well managed, whose decision makers follow sensible business practices, offer good products, and deal ethically and reliably with their suppliers, employees and customers.

If "like knows like" — and I believe this is arguably true — then moral people are better able to discern virtuous qualities that are not always casually apparent. Similarly, people of genuine and abiding faith tend to live out their beliefs daily, practice regular devotions, and conduct their lives with a degree of honorable self-discipline. This mode of living (which shows a certain parallel with the well run company) disposes someone to the patient attentiveness required for successful investment results over the long term. It also reflects an internalization of the idea of "stewardship," a recurring theme in the teachings of Christ. Someone who strives to be a faithful steward of family resources (or the resources of others) will be attuned to practical prospects and responsible choices, and naturally averse to flashy get-rich-quick schemes.

The down-side of faith as a characteristic of investors is that religious people may tend to look for the best in others even when cir-

11 *Centesimus Annas*, Section 19.

cumstances urge the opposite. The "Golden Rule" is not only about treating people justly, it also implies that we give others the benefit of the doubt. This can incline investors of faith to stick with failing companies even after alarm bells have begun sounding, or worse, subject them to the nefarious plottings of those who would exploit their good hearts. But of course, those dangers exist for non-believers as well. And when structures are in place to offer warning and provide proper guidance, the religious inclination to self-restraint gives faithful people an advantage.

In all these ways, then, religion conduces to prudent investing.

Is the obverse true? Could one claim that companies whose operations reflect a greater degree of moral concern are good investments? A corporation can be an extremely large, varied and complex creature, after all. Is the moral profile of its policies and practices relevant to its stock market performance? That isn't an easy question to answer, but certain factors are suggestive.

Good business management may not necessarily be a direct product of religious commitment, but it does correlate with ethical awareness, a decisively moral concept that has its roots in religious truth (i.e.: the Ten Commandments). Moreover, the values at the core of a company's operational approach — that particular set of objectives, priorities and working assumptions to which key decision makers must give assent — will ultimately find expression in the firm's public image. How often have you heard that XYZ Corp. doesn't care about its customers or that it treats its employees like dirt? Such are the building blocks of reputation, and reputation has a definite influence on investor attitudes toward any given stock. While it can't be indisputably claimed that religious principles drive share price, neither can the possibility of a cause-and-effect relationship between *values* and *value* be easily dismissed. As they say, "The truth will out."

In recent years, however, many investors have begun to look beyond the simple question of whether a corporation operates in an upright manner. There is a growing trend to apply ethical criteria to what companies are in the business of *doing*. When considering the purchase of a particular stock, they will ask more fundamental questions, such as: "Do I believe this company's products or services are *proper*? Is the business acceptable to me, personally, as a *legitimate* endeavor? Are its practices and procedures *right*?"

This kind of inquiry lifts investment decision making to a different level of concern, because it involves the element of *conscience*. And that is entirely appropriate, because when you acquire the stock of a corporation, you become one of the company's owners. This is true whether your shares are newly issued by the firm (perhaps in an initial public offering), or whether you have purchased existing shares through the secondary market of a stock exchange. It is equally true if you have inherited your shares or received them as a gift. Your ownership interest is real, it is significant, and it has the force of law behind it.

The reality of ownership is vividly illustrated when shareholders organize to complain that chronic poor performance by company management has caused the stock price to fall. The concept of the *proxy contest* is based on the fact that shareholders are owners with the right to express their views about company policies and procedures. (I wrote a book on the subject of proxy contests and how shareholders can exercise their influence.[12])

The company you own acts in your name, not only in delivering value as an investment by maintaining and improving its profitability, but in what it does on a daily basis. The one and only fiduciary responsibility which a board of directors has is to the investors who own the firm. As an owner, you have the legal right (actually, a responsibility) to act if directors fail in their duty to represent your interest.[13] At the same time, your status as an owner gives you certain ethical obligations as regards the policies and procedures by which the company operates.

---

12 *Shareholder Rebellion: How Investors are Changing the Way America's Companies are Run*, Irwin Professional Publishing, 1995.

13 Contrary to a very common misconception, corporate boards of directors have absolutely no fiduciary obligations to anybody other than their shareholders — not to a company's employees or its customers, or to the communities in which it operates, or to environmental activists, or to any other "stakeholder" (I hate that word). By law, a board's fiduciary responsibility is only to the company's owners.

There is, of course, a difference between legal and moral responsibility. The law of corporations protects individual shareholders from direct liability for the company's actions. Owning stock is not the same as being a partner. And that is an indispensable advantage to corporations in raising capital. The number of stock buyers would shrink to a tiny fraction of the current investing population if acquiring shares brought personal liability for business failures, loan defaults, or unpaid company bills.

As an investor, your participation in the corporate process is real and cannot be ignored. The amount of money you invest influences a company's current stock price, and impacts future price movements. It becomes part of the company's cumulative worth, helping to determine its financial viability, the level at which it can function, and its ability to raise future capital. The stocks you hold are not just claim checks on some possible future reward (like lottery tickets). They are real parts of real companies that produce real products and provide jobs for real people. Your investment portfolio is thus part of the economic life of the nation. It has power — power which is in your hands — and power is a distinctly moral concept.

The truth of this assertion has become clear to thousands of stockholders. Today there is a heightened awareness about the role played by personal investing in the free enterprise system. It has grown over recent decades, encouraged by such factors as the increasingly apparent failures and ultimate collapse of Communism as an alternative economic system; by the proliferation of mutual funds and the growing dominance of retirement plans in the financial markets (which has given more people than ever a direct stake in the ups and downs of Wall Street); and even by the increased hands-on investor involvement made possible by online trading.

Socially Responsible Investing

This stockholder awareness has coincided with the growth of numerous socially conscious movements, both domestic and international, which have sought to influence the business community in support of — or in opposition to — a variety of causes. The end of the apartheid regime in South Africa came about largely because stock-holders of major corporations and investors in important mutual funds were able to bring pressure on companies to *divest* themselves of their South African business holdings or to cut ties with other firms doing business in South Africa.

Likewise, motivated investors have played a significant role in putting race- and gender-equity issues on boardroom agendas, not to mention the environmentalist stockholder agitation that has assisted in prodding virtually all major U.S. corporations to "go green" (if, in some cases, more in their public relations pronouncements than in their actual operations). Indeed, company directors have come to expect pressure over policies and procedures, often in regard to issues that are quite peripheral to a firm's actual business. Annual meeting planners now take it pretty much as a given that some stockholder group will insist on floor time to promote one cause or another.

The rise of organized stockholder activism has been paralleled by the creation of financial products that enable individuals to express their social and political commitments through their stock purchases. A plentiful assortment of ideologically driven mutual funds has appeared on the scene under the label, "socially responsible investing". *Forbes* Magazine reported that, as of September 2008, there were 173 such funds, representing $172 billion in assets.[14]

The investment holdings of most such funds generally reflect judgments colored by social and political perspectives that would be termed "liberal" or "progressive." They tend to favor companies whose policies accord with the environmental, gender-sensitive, and social-justice concerns that find prominent expression in the foundation world, the mainstream media and entertainment industry, most college and university campuses, and the major not-for-profit organizations. Accordingly, corporate policies and procedures that allegedly "despoil the environment," "exploit oppressed minorities," "discrimi-

---

14 A quite thorough overview of socially responsible investing and funds created to reflect this concept can be found in the book, *Investing with your Values: Making Money and Making a Difference*, by Hal Brill, Jack A. Brill, and Cliff Feigenbaum, Bloomberg Press, 1999.

nate against women," "impede sustainable 'Third World' development," "contribute to international conflict," or create other situations of injustice (real or perceived) tend to rank highest among factors determining investment choices.

But if the liberal funds were earliest to market, investors with more conservative predilections — or who feel the tug of religious scruple in their financial thinking — are by no means without options. A parade of tradition-minded funds has passed across the stage in recent years, shorter perhaps than the liberal/progressive column, but of interesting variety. Investors who want a biblical (read "Evangelical Protestant") take on stock picking have been able to try the Timothy Plan, while those who mix national defense concerns with their Christian values have been offered the Patriot Fund. The Amana Growth Fund, designed specifically for Muslim investors, factors Islamic principles into its stock-analysis matrix, while Catholics have sampled the eponymously named Catholic Funds, along with the Aquinas Funds, the Epiphany Funds, and the fund family I created, the Ave Maria Mutual Funds.

Morally Responsible Investing

Just because an investment plan has a religious flavor or touts a church connection, you shouldn't assume that it is markedly different from the general run of "socially responsible" offerings. The Presbyterian-affiliated New Covenant Mutual Funds, for instance, reflect their denomination's generally liberal affinities, and the criteria for selecting stocks are virtually indistinguishable from any number of secular funds without an ideological focus.

In this book I wish to acquaint you with a very specific approach to religiously based investing — one that is motivated by faith and is guided by a particular set of ethical precepts. I call it Morally Responsible Investing.

While "socially responsible investing" (SRI) addresses a broad spectrum of economic, political and environmental issues, Morally Responsible Investing (MRI) focuses specifically on making investment decisions that embrace key areas of human concern. Overshadowing every other consideration is the sanctity of life. Protecting life from the moment of conception is the *sine qua non* of all human concern. If children are not born, there can be no other human concern. Following close on the sanctity of life is the inviolability of marriage.

Any number of other issues are important and may make legitimate claims upon our compassion, charity, and personal commitment. But the sanctity of life and the inviolability of marriage constitute the basis of our being and our human uniqueness. They have profound implications for the health and wellbeing of the human community. They go to the essence of *family* — the very foundation of every civilization, every cultural movement, every religion in human history. That's why this pair of concerns has always received special attention in the Judeo-Christian moral tradition (particularly in the moral theology of the Catholic Church). In addition, they have undeniable economic implications. Family security, provision for spouses, and the future wellbeing of children are at the heart of most personal investment decisions. They even provide much of the impetus for building businesses.

Of course, to speak of such concepts as "the sanctity of life and the inviolability of marriage" is to court controversy these days. Truths about human nature and human relationships which were once accepted as self-evident have become fighting words. And to attach such ideas to investing is to risk responses that go well beyond raised eyebrows or the blank stare of perplexity.

Every election cycle, religious people (especially Catholics) are treated to a barrage of specious arguments attempting to justify the pro-abortion votes of politicians who claim to be earnest adherents of their various faiths. For instance, the last campaign season (2008) saw an attempt on the part of House Speaker Nancy Pelosi to convince her fellow Catholics that the Church has been somehow ambivalent in opposing abortion over the centuries and so her own pro-abortion views fit well within the spectrum of legitimate Catholic opinion. The Speaker's comments brought forth a storm of corrective teaching from the bishops,[15] perhaps the most earnest and concerted blast of catechetics to be heard from U.S. Church leaders in quite some time. Pelosi backed off quickly.

Try as they might to kick up dust around the topic, abortion advocates cannot obscure the obvious fact that abortion is the taking of innocent human life. Whether or not there are situations that justify abortion is a question which has been debated since the beginning of time, and that debate will likely always be with us. But abortion kills babies. That is the gross and brutal truth which simply cannot be prettied up. Moreover, the legality of abortion pollutes the moral atmosphere of society in general. If it is permissible to slaughter the most helpless and innocent among us, then on what ethical basis can we prohibit any other harmful act? The acceptance of abortion thus throws law itself into question, weakening the moral foundation of our entire culture. So if you seek to invest in a way that is morally responsible, the starting point has to be avoiding companies that participate in or provide support for abortion, as well as any mutual funds that have the shares of complicit companies among their holdings.

Closely connected with abortion is the subject of artificial birth control. Catholic teaching prohibits the use of chemical or mechanical devices that interfere with conception. Also prohibited is *in vitro* fertilization.

Most non-Catholic religious communities diverge from the Catholic standard on this issue, as do most individual Catholics, for that matter. But life has surprising ways of vindicating the Catholic view (as articulated by Pope Paul VI in the 1968 encyclical, *Humane*

---

15 The victory of abortion advocate Barack Obama —made possible in part by strong electoral support among Catholics — touched a nerve in the American hierarchy. A post-election statement from the United States Conference of Catholic Bishops included an ominous warning to the president-elect about the national divisiveness he would be courting in a single-minded pursuit of expanded "abortion rights." Issued on November 13, 2008, less than two weeks after the election, the statement noted that, "Abortion kills not only unborn children; it destroys constitutional order and the common good, which is assured only when the life of every human being is legally protected."

Vitae[16]). This was made all too clear with the January 2009 birth of octuplets to a southern California woman through embryo implantation.

Unmarried and with six children already, 33-year-old Nadya Suleman had received treatment at a Beverly Hills fertility clinic apparently out of an insatiable craving for motherhood (though her own mother put it somewhat more colorfully, claiming that Nadya is "obsessed with children").[17]

This is only one of the more extreme examples of a persistent desire to assert human dominance over the natural processes of life. Octo-mom aside, the real story on fertility is that it's falling to levels

---

16 *Humanae Vitae* states in Section 17 that "we must accept that there are certain limits, beyond which it is wrong to go, to the power of man over his own body and its natural functions — limits, let it be said, which no one, whether as a private individual or as a public authority, can lawfully exceed."

17 This incident drew surprisingly wide criticism in a society as ethically challenged as ours has become. Reaction was negative even in open-minded southern California. On February 11, 2009, *Los Angeles Times* writer Tim Rutten published a blistering commentary, observing what he termed the "manifest irresponsibility of this eccentric woman toward her children" as well as "the irresponsibility of the physician who took money to impregnate a jobless, husbandless woman with 14 children."

Rutten asserted that the case illustrates "the complexities that arise when people assume that because something can be done, it should be done." He offered this cogent (if sarcastic) insight: "The impulse that has made fertility medicine such a large and lucrative specialty in American medicine is about something other than children; it's about the narcissistic assumption that one is 'entitled' to 'the experience' of childbearing and, more to the point, the notion that, somehow, if your particular strands of DNA don't live on into another generation, the species will be poorer for it."

Even syndicated columnist Ellen Goodman, of the *Boston Globe*, a writer who rarely encounters an example of human (especially feminist) self-absorption with which she can't sympathize, grasped the ethical implications. "Does anyone have a right to tell anyone else how many kids to have?" her column of February 6 asked. "Can only people who can afford them bear children? Do you need a husband to have a baby? These are questions that make us feel queasy when we are talking about old-fashioned families. But they take on a new flavor in the unregulated wild west of fertility technology."

Not unexpectedly, Goodman took her sharpest jab at the medical establishment. As she wrote, "a reproductive business that generates so much controversy has produced a remarkable consensus. Infertility treatment for an unemployed, single mother of six? Eight embryos in one womb? There must be a proper word in the medical literature to describe this achievement. I think the word is 'nuts.'"

that have economic implications sufficient to pose a genuine threat to human wellbeing. And it's a global phenomenon; conservative commentator, Don Feder, who writes and speaks frequently on population issues, has noted:

> Humanity is failing to reproduce itself in sufficient numbers to maintain our civilization.
>
> In this regard, one number is crucial — 2.1. That's the number of children the average woman must have in her lifetime just to maintain current population. This is known as a replacement-level birth rate.
>
> In 30 years, worldwide, birth rates have fallen by more than 50 percent. In 1979, the average woman on this planet had 6 children. Today, the average is 2.9 children, and falling. According to the United Nations Population Division, by the middle of this century, worldwide fertility will be below replacement.[18]

The subject of lopsided demographics often comes up in discussions of how the Social Security system can survive when numbers of the elderly retired overwhelm those of the working young. But the dangers of population imbalance touch far more than that. The ever-shrinking numbers of babies undermines the fundamental expectation of economic growth, which undeniably bears on investing.[19]

---

18 Feder's dispiriting picture of population decline is laid out in a presentation he gives at pro-life events, such as the 36th annual March for Life Rose Dinner held January 22, 2009 in Washington. His text is archived on line at: http://www.lifesitenews.com/ldn/2009_docs/DonFederRoseDinnerspeech.pdf.

19 The urgency of the situation received special emphasis in January 2009, when Austrian chemist Carl Djerassi, one of three scientists whose research led to formulation of the synthetic progestagen, Norethisterone, a critical step in development of the first oral contraceptive, published a commentary in the Austrian newspaper, *Der Standard*, in which he described the "horror scenario" of population decline brought on by birth control. The 85-year-old retired researcher called the fall in birth rates an "epidemic" that is more of a threat to civic health than obesity. He wrote that couples trying to avoid reproducing themselves were merely "wanting to enjoy their schnitzels while leaving the rest of the world to get on with it." A report by the Catholic News Agency noting Djerassi's commentary is archived online at: http://www.catholicnewsagency.com/new.php?n=14730.

Companies that advance technologies that interfere with natural life processes risk the constriction of those very markets on which their own products and services depend. As Archbishop Charles Chaput of Denver has observed, "The future of a community, a people, a church, and a nation depends on the children who will inherit it. If we prevent our children from being born, we remove ourselves from the future. It's really that simple. No children, no future."[20, 21]

Argue with Church teaching if you like. Say the bishops are out of step with the current sexual ethos. They will readily agree that they are, and of course, that's the point. But to be fully consistent with the Catholic moral vision, a conscientious investor would avoid companies that support fertility manipulation in ways similar to those involved with abortion.

The other great leg upon which Morally Responsible Investing stands is the sanctity of marriage. When you think about the sanctity of marriage, the first word that comes to mind is "divorce." It would be hard to identify companies that have a direct financial interest in the break-up of marriages (other than, perhaps, the publisher of

20 This truth was illustrated with chilling astuteness by British writer, P.D. James, whose novel, *The Children of Men*, was set in a bleak world where all of humanity had suddenly ceased to be fertile.

21 It must be acknowledged that there is disagreement, not only about the danger posed by population decline, but over whether it is actually happening at all. Since the English political economist Thomas Robert Malthus (1766-1834) first put forth his theory that population growth would eventually outpace food production (what's termed the "Malthusian Catastrophe"), overpopulation has been a persistent fear. The idea was given dramatic expression in the 1968 book, *The Population Bomb*, by Paul Ehrlich, currently of Stanford University. It persists today primarily as an argument for that Holy Grail of the environmental movement, "sustainability."

Paul Ehrlich was one of the founders of the group, Zero Population Growth (now called Population Connection), which has been a principal advocate of so-called "reproductive rights." Its British counterpart, the Optimum Population Trust, recently launched an initiative aimed at convincing people to have fewer children, known as "Stop at Two." It is now widely acknowledged that, except in certain confined geographic localities, overpopulation is a myth. Though his academic specialty is entomology, the study of insects, Ehrlich is the "go-to guy" for media folks writing on population issues. He may be an expert on bug life, but as a demographic prophet he has proven to be a quack (as was Malthus before him).

Divorce Magazine, which is a real periodical[22]). Of course, there are plenty of law firms that specialize in divorce, but law firms tend to be partnerships, rather than corporations, and so don't have stock which outside investors can buy.

I suppose one could argue that a lot of companies make demands on their employees which put stress on marriages. But work-related stress can have many other effects beside harming marriages (such as breakdown in health), and for all practical purposes, it would be impossible to use divorce statistics as an investment-screening criterion.

Other things assault the sanctity of marriage, however, and the one most directly connected with the subject of investing is *pornography*. American society is awash in salacious images and sex-drenched entertainment. What used to be confined to the back-street peepshows and dirty book stalls is now everyday fare. Here again, the words of Pius XI are relevant:

> "We must not omit to mention those crafty men who, wholly unconcerned about any honest usefulness of their work, do not scruple to stimulate the baser human desires and, when they are aroused, use them for their own profit."[23]

Most hardcore material comes out of privately held production firms, some associated with organized crime. Corporations like Playboy Enterprises account for their portion of smut as well, and the case for their exclusion is obvious. What might not be top-of-mind when thinking about porn is that the overwhelming portion of questionable matter is in the hands of America's most prominent communications firms. I'm talking about cable and satellite television operators, Internet service providers, some of the largest periodical publishers and distributors, even phone companies. Add to that the video rental chains, hospitality firms offering on-demand "adult" fare in

---

22 *Divorce Magazine* is published by the Toronto-based Segue Esprit Inc., which also operates Divorce Marketing Group, a firm offering services to attorneys and other professionals involved in divorce throughout the United States and Canada.

23 *Quadragesimo Anno*, Paragraph 132.

hotel rooms, and some of the leading big-box and shopping-mall retailers, and you begin to grasp the scope of the pornography market and the challenge involved in avoiding porn-related investments. These organizations are at the core of mainstreaming pornography and dulling society's sense of propriety.

Some people will tell you that porn is so profitable and pervasive that it's nigh well impossible to screen out of your investments, so you might as well cash in on the earnings opportunity it represents.[24] I know of at least two investment books touting vice-related stocks (pornography, gambling, alcohol and others) as sure-fire winners in just about any market.[25] There are undoubtedly more.

Actually, pornography isn't all that secure as an industry. In recent years, the biggest operators have found themselves under competitive pressure. Their lock on the video market, in particular, has been weakened by low-cost digital recorders that allow amateur "artistes" all over the world to produce and flood the Internet with their own "skin flicks" — of lesser quality than professional fare, perhaps, but available for download free. Thus, digital technology is doing to porn what it did to the record companies and mainstream movie producers. Old-line suppliers are scrambling to come up with a new business model, the ultimate shape of which remains to be seen.

The pornography business has also suffered under recession, just like other industries. In January 2009, Larry Flynt, founder of the notorious *Hustler* magazine, issued a press statement putting forth a rationale for government bailout. "With all this economic misery and people losing all that money, sex is the farthest thing from their mind," he wrote. "It's time for congress to rejuvenate the sexual appetite of

---

24 The February 2008 issue of the conservative Catholic journal, *New Oxford Review*, illustrates the ubiquitousness of pornography-related investments, noting that Christian Brothers Investment Services, which manages funds for more than 1,000 U.S. Catholic dioceses and Church-related institutions, was holding shares in Lodgenet, "one of the largest providers of in-room porn to the hotel industry."

25 *Stocking Up on Sin: How to Crush the Market with Vice-Based Investing*, by Caroline Wexler, John Wiley & Sons, Inc. (2004); and *Investing in Vice: The Recession-Proof Portfolio of Booze, Bets, Bombs, and Butts*, by Dan Ahrens, St. Martin's Press (2004).

America. The only way they can do this is by supporting the adult industry and doing it quickly."

One feels for poor Larry Flynt, that indefatigable self-promoter. But then it brings to mind the old Depression-era saying: "Things are tough all over."

Still, the pervasiveness of porn and the new-found success of the amateurs only emphasizes the strong appeal of erotic entertainment. Preoccupation with vicarious sexual thrills can become a genuine addiction that intrudes on the relationship of husband and wife, diverts attention from essential human ties, and ultimately risks the destruction of marriage and family life. It's not only men who are susceptible. Mental health professionals and family counselors are reporting dramatic increases in porn involvement among women (those bodice-ripping romance novels are only the tip of the iceberg).

Porn has even become a prominent part of teenage life. High school girls have pioneered a whole new genre of prurient self-expression — "sexting" — the practice of photographing themselves in provocative poses and various states of undress, then sharing their works with friends via cell phones and online social networking. This has led to teenagers around the country being charged with distribution of child pornography. Several face the prospect of being listed on sex-offender registries.

Thus, the danger to impressionable youngsters of our society's pervasive atmosphere of hyper-eroticism is self-evident. "Better the millstone," as the Lord said.

With such cultural conditions — fostered by a profound misreading and distorted enforcement of the First Amendment —individuals feel there's little they can do to reverse our society's slide into the muck. But for investors, one bit of positive action is available: avoiding the stock, not only of companies that produce porn, but those that provide the means by which it permeates modern life. Therefore, screening for pornography involvement must be considered a key component of any investment plan which can be judged morally responsible.

We have the power and therefore the obligation to take a stand against Pius XI's "crafty men."

chapter 2

In the Beginning

I may be the world's most enthusiastic proponent of Morally Responsible Investing, but I have to admit that MRI was not my idea. There have been times during my career when I declined an opportunity to purchase a certain stock because I disliked the firm's practices (there were other times when I held my nose and bought anyway, because the numbers were just too attractive to ignore). But I had never tried to combine securities analysis with moral judgment in any systematic way. In fact, I was skeptical about funds created for the purpose of investing "responsibly." For me, social responsibility and stock market return were two distinctly different issues. I held the common view that a company's duty is to deliver profit to its shareholders, who are free to support whatever charitable initiatives or social objectives they like — one having nothing to do with the other.

That view was challenged in a serious way one morning in January of 2001. Tom Monaghan, the well known businessman and philanthropist, invited me to a meeting at the headquarters of the Ave Maria Foundation, an organization he had established to pursue his interest in Catholic education and evangelism. Also in attendance was Bowie Kuhn, former Commissioner of Major League Baseball and a Catholic layman active in a wide variety of Church-related projects. I had managed investments for both of these gentlemen over the years, and had always admired their commitment to our shared faith and the causes that touched their hearts. They put a proposition to me which at first left me quite confused. They wanted me to start a Catholic mutual fund.

"What exactly is a Catholic mutual fund?" I asked.

While I was aware that funds with religious affiliations existed, I had never been involved with one. In what kinds of companies would a Catholic mutual fund invest — firms that made religious goods, (crucifixes, rosaries and the like), or publishers of Bibles and catechetical books, or construction companies that specialized in building churches and parochial schools? The concept of "Catholic investing" seemed rather limited.

Tom and Bowie found my befuddled expression quite amusing. They had both been serving on the advisory board of a fund called the Catholic Values Investment Trust.[1] CVIT had assets of about $30 million under management, a large portion of which was Tom's money. While it was supposed to reflect "Catholic values," its managers selected investments according to criteria typical of most "socially responsible" funds. And according to Tom and Bowie, the people running CVIT weren't terribly consistent with those. It seems to have been a common practice to waive the restrictions for attractive stocks that didn't quite meet the fund's stated screening guidelines.

This did not sit well with either Tom or Bowie, who had gotten involved in CVIT with *reformist* expectations. They were seeking a purer investing approach, and over several months began roughing out the idea of a fund in which anyone (Catholics or non-Catholics) could invest, but that would examine stocks from the specific perspective of Catholic moral teaching. Such a fund, they told me, might be designed like the Schwartz Value Fund (which my brother, Greg, and I had been operating for 17 years at that time), seeking out the best companies in any field — except that it would not buy shares of firms supporting abortion.

---

1   The Catholic Values Investment Trust would later be merged into the Catholic Equity Fund, run by the Catholic Knights, which with about 85,000 members, is the second largest Catholic fraternal organization (after the Knights of Columbus).

Their idea was simple and, actually, rather thought-provoking: *If you're against abortion and understand how destructive it is to our social fabric, what can you do about it? You could make a placard and walk up and down the street. You could put up a billboard or buy time on a radio station to express your view. You could give money to pro-life organizations. But how much could you really hope to accomplish by individual action? On the other hand, if you got a group of like-minded, motivated people together, what could you accomplish collectively? Since we live in a capitalistic society, perhaps you could channel people's intentions and resources into a mutual fund that might actually have the ability to change corporate behavior. In that way you could possibly have a significant impact.*

An interesting premise — even if it struck me as rather overly optimistic. I didn't dismiss the idea out of hand, however. Instead, I threw a thought of my own back at them. "Changing corporate behavior is a laudable goal," I said. "But it seems to me that such an objective would have to be pretty far down the road. To get people to invest today, starting from scratch, you'd need a more modest and clearly defined mission. Still, a fund such as you're suggesting could at least give people a means to invest in a manner consistent with their faith."

That thought reframed the idea in a way I could grasp. Because it was evident to me that faith, particularly *Catholic* faith, provided a definite set of ethical precepts to guide the decision-making required in managing such a fund, a clear set of criteria by which stocks could be selected. A fund based on Catholic moral philosophy — that vast and elaborate edifice of scholarship and wisdom constructed over centuries and validated by the Magisterium (teaching authority) of the Church — would have a degree of substance and legitimacy unmatched in an ideology-driven fund with the generalized intent of "saving the planet" or "creating equal opportunity" or "ending exploitation" or any other nebulous objective of "social responsibility." The concept began to seem valid, and quite intriguing, all the more so because of what I knew about Tom Monaghan.

Adventures with Tom

I first met Tom in 1976 through my wife, Judi. She had gotten acquainted with him at the University of Notre Dame, where they were both part of a group that had come from Ann Arbor, Michigan, to participate in a retreat on campus. Tom had achieved regional celebrity status because of his success with Domino's Pizza, the food-service company he'd founded a decade-and-a-half earlier. During a dinner Tom was hosting for all the retreatants (at a pizza parlor near Notre Dame, since he made it a practice to check out the competition), Judi happened to mention that her husband was an investment counselor. This apparently piqued Tom's interest, and he said he'd like to meet me.

An opportunity presented itself soon after, when Judi and I ran into him at a fund-raiser for Ann Arbor's Father Gabriel Richard Catholic High School. Judi introduced us, and we got into an extended chat. I was surprised at how similar our views were on a range of topics. We were both practicing Catholics who'd had a conservative (or as they say now, "orthodox") upbringing in the Church, though Tom seemed considerably more devout than me. Politically we were of a similar mind, both Republicans and intolerant of the liberalism which we agreed (with unapologetic conviction) was "spreading like a cancer" throughout society. Both of us were sports enthusiasts; in 1984 Tom would buy the Detroit Tigers baseball team. In essence, we hit it off right from the start.

Thus began a long and fruitful association. Some years later, Tom would invite me to attend the weekly breakfasts held at Domino's Farms, headquarters of his pizza company, by a Catholic men's group organized a few years earlier. The Tuesday-morning gatherings began with 7:00 a.m. Mass and included guest breakfast speakers addressing various topics of inspirational interest. I found the presentations engaging and the camaraderie of fellow Catholic men uplifting (I still attend as often as I can).

Even the setting was interesting. In contrast to its rustic name, Domino's Farms is a thoroughly modern, architecturally distinctive, and *huge* (more than a million square feet in space and nearly a kilometer in length) multi-tenant office park, designed in the famous "Prairie Style" of Frank Lloyd Wright. The *farm* aspect is provided by the surroundings, which include fields under active cultivation and rolling pastures populated by specialty breeds of cattle along with a herd of north American bison. There's also Domino's Petting Farm, an agricultural exhibition and teaching facility that draws families and school groups from around the area. (The pairing of rural life and Frank Lloyd Wright reflects Tom's interests and personal history. Long a Wright enthusiast, Tom had wanted to be an architect before being lured onto a different path by the pizza business, and he spent part of his childhood living on a farm.[2])

My contacts with Tom continued, both in and out of the men's breakfasts. Over the years, I had numerous opportunities to watch him in action, both in his business dealings and in his personal relationships. I was impressed with his kindness and generosity, and benefited from it myself. Once in 1992, he made arrangements for me to use his personal box at Detroit's Tiger Stadium to entertain some clients. He had just sold the team to Mike Ilitch, founder of the rival pizza chain, Little Caesar's. This was, in fact, the very last night the box was under Tom's control. My clients and I were treated royally, fed to bursting with Domino's products, which the waiter who served us explained made us something of a footnote in Detroit baseball history. This was the last time Domino's Pizza would be served. Beginning the next day, the fare would be Little Caesar's.

As it happened, a short time after that experience, Harry Silverman, Domino's Pizza Vice President of Finance, called me about looking into some investments, both for the pizza company and for Tom personally. I made an appointment for Harry to come to my firm's headquarters, located about 30 miles from Ann Arbor in Bloomfield Hills, one of Detroit's northern suburbs. On the day of our appointment he showed up with two colleagues, Paul Roney, who then

---

2   The story of Tom's rather tumultuous upbringing, his business travails, and his wildly eclectic interests can be found in his autobiography, *Pizza Tiger*, published by Random House (1986).

was treasurer of Domino's, and Mike Marcantonio, a CPA and tax specialist for the company (and, incidentally, Tom's son-in-law, married to daughter, Maggie). The three toured our offices, meeting all of my analysts and portfolio managers. They asked extensive questions about our investment philosophy, our track record, and how we might be able to help Tom and Domino's with their investment needs. They must have been impressed with what they learned, because a week later they transferred a multi-million-dollar account to Schwartz Investment Counsel, Inc. My firm has managed investments for the Monaghan Family ever since.[3]

During the 1980s and early '90s, Tom had become increasingly immersed in charitable activities, especially projects involving the Church. He founded Legatus, the international Catholic business leaders fraternal organization, established private Catholic elementary schools in the Ann Arbor area and mission schools in Central America, and underwrote construction of a new cathedral in Managua, Nicaragua, to replace one that had been destroyed in an earthquake. Also in those years, Domino's was experiencing a series of wild fluctuations in its business fortunes. It came near to collapse in 1992, then recovered dramatically, and over the next six years achieved some of its greatest successes.

The stresses of business were beginning to weigh on Tom, and his heart was, more and more, drawn to his faith-related enterprises. So much so that he decided to sell the company. In 1998, Tom accepted

---

3   Another long-standing connection with the Monaghan family involves my wife, Judi, who volunteered in the Development Office at Father Gabriel Richard High School, working closely with Tom's daughter, Susie. Judi became involved at FGRHS shortly after introducing me to Tom, and my taking him and Domino's Pizza on as clients, working at the school, on average, three to four days a week over the course of some 13 years. She and Susie became close friends during that time, and their relationship has continued.

    In tribute to Judi, who is truly selfless in her efforts on behalf of causes in which she believes — always choosing to toil humbly behind the scenes — I should mention that she helped in raising millions of dollars for the school, and received praise from Development Director Jane Dorr on many occasions. But that's my wife, whom I regard as a genuine unsung heroine.

an offer of approximately $1 billion in a leveraged buyout from the private equity firm Bain Capital (at the time, run by Mitt Romney).

Such a substantial infusion of cash gave Tom the wherewithal to let his charitable instincts run wild, and a series of innovative, Catholic-themed start-ups and acquisitions soon followed in rapid succession. Tom founded Ave Maria Institute, a post-secondary school that was the first step in the development of Ave Maria College and, later, Ave Maria University. He hired a former Michigan public prosecutor, Richard Thompson, who had gained fame for his battle with physician-assisted suicide advocate, Jack Kevorkian (the notorious "Dr. Death"), to start the Thomas More Law Center, a Catholic public-interest law firm specializing in pro-life and religious-liberty issues. He then lured Bernard Dobranski, dean of the law school at Catholic University of America, away from that venerable institution to start Ave Maria School of Law in Ann Arbor.

Casting his philanthropic net over a wide stretch of Catholic life, Tom acquired an interest in Catholic Singles Online, a digital match-making service, changing the name to Ave Maria Singles. He bought and invested in several Michigan AM radio stations and started Ave Maria Radio, a media-communications firm that is now the leading source of original Catholic radio programming in the nation (and a major program provider to the EWTN Global Catholic Radio service, the audio arm of Mother Angelica's Eternal Word Television Network). And there was much more, including the underwriting of a new order of nuns, the Dominican Sisters of Mary, Mother of the Eucharist, to operate the Catholic elementary schools he funded (that order has since become one of the fastest-growing communities of Religious women in the world).

Subsequent years have seen several of his undertakings succeed brilliantly. Some have had their day and faded into the mists of lay Catholic history. For others, the jury is still out. Nevertheless, with Tom's multi-faceted business background, his track record of faith-based entrepreneurship, and his activist bent, it made sense that he would eventually see investing as a vehicle of reform.

Still, despite my experience with Tom (and for all of Bowie Kuhn's devotion to the concept), I was unsure about the marketability of a Catholic mutual fund — though I was now quite intrigued by the notion. I told them I would give serious thought to the idea and get back to them with my decision about whether or not I wished to become involved. My first step in undertaking that serious thought was to consult my wife.

Judi is a very balanced person who sees things from a sensible perspective, but from a point of view that's distinct from my own. Her middle name is Pearl, and she has proven to be my "Pearl of Great Value"[4] over more than four decades of marriage. Judi listened as I recounted my meeting with Tom and Bowie and described their idea. She pondered the notion of a Catholic mutual fund, and then, very logically and cogently, laid out a series of questions that were different from the things I had been thinking about: (1) "What would be required of you in running such a fund?" (2) "How would it transform your investment practice?" (3) "What are the opportunities and risks involved?"

I didn't have answers to any of them. In fact, I realized that the answers probably wouldn't be obtainable for some time — not until after preparations for such a fund were well underway, in all likelihood. But Judi's questions helped me to envision the scope of this task which Tom and Bowie wanted me to take on. I began to see that the implications for my professional life were extensive.

Judi may have sensed some anxiety stirring within me (and the need for some countervailing reassurance). "Well," she said, "you know Tom and Bowie. You know they're honest, they're good businessmen, and they're faithful Catholics." And then she added playfully,

---

4   As in Jesus' parable about the man who sold everything he had in order to possess the one object whose value was beyond measure. Judi and I met in high school and married soon after college. I was introduced to her by a mutual friend, Marcia (Walker) Byrnes, who told me, "You'll like Judi Arnold. She's the smartest girl at Immaculata High School, and also the best athlete." Marcia was right, and I shall be forever grateful to her. Marcia remained a close friend until her death from cancer in 2005.

"Besides, they're both devoted to the Blessed Mother, so how bad could a mutual fund called 'Ave Maria' be?"

In her way, Judi provided me with the impetus I needed to really explore the idea. If her reaction had been negative, I probably would have gone no further. But I dove into some basic research. In 2001 there were approximately 60 million Catholics in the U.S., of which roughly half were adults. At least 6 million of those were investors, and various studies of Church attendance suggested that 1.2 million could be considered "orthodox" (that is, regular Mass-goers active in their parishes, pro-life, holding traditional moral views, and faithful to the Magisterium of the Church). This was our primary market, 1,200,000 "orthodox" Catholics. Beyond those were as many other investors as we could induce to consider the validity of a mutual fund with our proposed moral restraints (including non-Catholics of pro-life disposition) — and who knew how many of those there might be? Well, I thought, 1.2 million wasn't a bad number to start with. I told Tom and Bowie I'd give it a try.

Getting Started

The first question which would have to be answered was: *Is a Catholic mutual fund legal?* I turned to our Washington D.C. law firm, Sullivan and Worcester, whose investment specialists advised that such a device could pass muster with the Securities and Exchange Commission (SEC), as long as we made appropriate disclosure of the fund's religious character in the prospectus, specifying the purpose of the fund and what kinds of companies we planned to avoid in our stock-selection process. Basically, the Sullivan attorneys told us that the SEC would view our Catholic moral perspective in the way it viewed the screening criteria of "socially responsible" funds — as an idiosyncrasy.

Having confirmed that our fund idea was legal, the challenge we faced next was how to give the concept some *materiality* — in other words how to make it seem like something more than just an interesting notion floating around in the imaginations of three reform-minded Catholics (which was really all it was at that point). The obvious way to make it credible was to entice some high-profile Catholic figures into lending their names to the project. We were extremely fortunate to find several prominent people who grasped our premise, understood its potential, and were willing to attach their own reputations to it in a very public way.

First to sign on was the famous scholar, theologian and author, Michael Novak. He was joined by Phyllis Schlafly, the pro-life/pro-family activist and founder of the conservative Eagle Forum, along with Thomas J. Sullivan, a retired executive of McGraw-Hill (and a shirt-tail relative of mine by marriage). Paul Roney, who had gone on to serve as executive director of Tom's Ave Maria Foundation after the sale of Domino's Pizza, was added, not only to strengthen the Ave Maria connection, but to lend his personal credibility as a CPA. Adam Cardinal Maida, at that time Archbishop of Detroit, agreed to serve as our Ecclesiastic Advisor. Then, through Bowie Kuhn's vast web of personal connections — and, frankly, much to my surprise — we were able to snag Larry Kudlow, former Wall Street economist and now a popular market commentator, host of the "Kudlow Report" on cable network, CNBC. When we'd approached him, I hadn't actually expected that such a visible figure would be willing to lend support to so new and unusual an enterprise. Tom and Bowie, themselves, rounded out the panel, Bowie taking up duties as chairman.

Assembling this group of distinguished individuals gave us a foundation on which to begin building and promoting the fund. But it did something else, as well, it widened the focus of the screening process we would develop. With Cardinal Maida's advice, the advisory board recommended that we make contributions to Planned Parenthood a specific criterion for excluding a company's stock. The board also decided to exclude companies that produced or distributed pornography, as well as those that provided non-marital partner benefits to their employees (though that last criterion would raise questions which we would find ourselves having to address in the future).

This process of refining the definition of what we intended to offer investors helped to sharpen our ethical vision. The Board felt it made the fund a more comprehensive reflection of Catholic moral teaching, and solidified the concept of Morally Responsible Investing. To me, personally, it made the project real in a way it hadn't been before. For the first time I began to believe that Tom and Bowie's idea had genuine prospects.

Getting our application cleared by the SEC proved a challenge — and something of an education. I had expected that a Catholic mutual fund might be viewed with a certain skepticism by government regulators accustomed to the *values-neutral* approach that dominates investment thinking on Wall Street. What I didn't expect to encounter was an apparent anti-Catholic bias.

The SEC staff member handling our application kept sending it back to us with what, in most cases, appeared to be nit-picking objections. Our lawyers repeatedly redrafted the document to make it acceptable, and on each resubmission still more changes were required. My first assumption was that we were dealing with an attitude that is unfortunately common among some government employees, a mindset that combines boredom with self-importance. But the objections gradually began to assume a pattern that suggested there might be some personal distaste for a mutual fund with a Catholic flavor. I confronted the individual, and my suspicion was confirmed by a remark that was as ignorant as it was snide: "If you're going to have a cardinal serving as your advisor, why not just get him to put his imprimatur on the fund?" That an imprimatur is only applied to books demonstrated the ignorance. The tone with which this remark was made accounted for the rest of my impression.

I was outraged. But my attorney offered the nearest thing to consolation I was likely to get under the circumstances, that well worn bit of folk wisdom: "You can't fight City Hall."

Was all this delay just the inertia endemic to government bureaucracy, or was there actual anti-Catholic bias involved? Was Tom's connection with the fund a factor? Tom Monaghan has attracted much attention, and no small amount of criticism, for his support of certain candidates and political causes, generally of the conservative variety. Even though our dealings with the SEC took place during the George W. Bush administration, which with its interest in faith-based initiatives, was disposed to applaud his efforts (and quick to put the arm on him for campaign money), we still ran up against the iron rule of government: "Administrations come and go; bureaucracy is forever."

My suspicions about bias aside, the processing of our application took a positively mystical turn. The Ave Maria Catholic Values Fund was approved on a beautiful spring day, May 1st — May Day — the day of Our Lady (the phrase, "Ave Maria," of course, is Latin for "Hail Mary"). It brought back memories of May crownings from my 1950s childhood as a pupil in Detroit's Precious Blood School. If I'd had any lingering uncertainties about whether the idea of a Catholic mutual fund was valid, they were all completely dispelled now. Clearly, the Lord was working in His own good time. My colleagues and I were ecstatic.

Putting It All Together

The actual organizing of the first Ave Maria Mutual Fund was quite easy. We had an existing fiduciary structure in the Schwartz Investment Trust, under whose umbrella the Ave Maria Catholic Values Fund was established. We also had a proven Value Investing template to follow in the Schwartz Value Fund, in operation since 1984. It was a simple matter to integrate the new fund into arrangements already in place.[5] Sullivan and Worcester, our law firm of long standing, became the fund's counsel-of-record. Deloitte and Touche became our auditors, U.S. Bank our fund custodian, and Ultimus Fund Solutions our transfer agent, fund accounting agent, and fund administrator.

---

5   The board of trustees for the Schwartz Investment Trust took on fiduciary responsibilities for the Ave Maria Catholic Values Fund. Board members at that time were: Donald J. Dawson, Jr., Fred A. Erb, John J. McHale, and Sidney F. McKenna, along with Bowie Kuhn, my brother, Gregory J. Schwartz, and myself.

From the outset, I determined that we would offer a *no-load* fund — which is to say, there would be no up-front commissions (customarily 3 to 5 percent). This ran counter to advice I received from several brokerage houses that insisted they would be much more inclined to offer a new fund such as ours if they got commissions at the time their customers bought in. The front-loading of mutual funds has always gone against my grain. I feel strongly that every dollar an investor puts into a fund should go to buy shares of the fund — not 95 or 97 cents of that dollar, but *all* of it. The Schwartz Value Fund had always been a no-load fund, and the Ave Maria Catholic Values Fund would be, too.

Naturally, as with all mutual funds, there would have to be internal management fees paid to a registered investment adviser, in this case that being Schwartz Investment Counsel, Inc. — my company — for the research, analysis, stock screening, portfolio management, and administrative services that make up the professional investing process. But those fees, currently ranging from 30 to 100 basis points (a basis point representing 1/100th of 1 percent), are normal fund expenses, not any kind of toll investors must pay to participate. This, it has always seemed to me, is the only fair way to operate. The effort we put in as managers is what makes the fund succeed. That effort has value. As Jesus said, "The workman deserves his wage."

Without up-front commissions to encourage broker sales, we decided to take the Ave Maria Catholic Values Fund directly to potential investors ourselves. We secured the services of a Boston-area advertising agency, Clerestory Communications, and launched an aggressive campaign in Catholic media, built around the simple, direct theme: "Smart Investing and Catholic Values." The agency bought ads in such national Catholic magazines as *Our Sunday Visitor*, *St. Anthony Messenger*, and *Catholic Digest*, as well as on Catholic radio (in particular, the nationally syndicated talk show, "Kresta in the Afternoon") and in some of the more important diocesan papers (*Catholic Digest*, with a circulation in excess of 300,000, performed best of all Catholic media).

We also experimented with selected general and business publications, including *Time, Newsweek,* and *Business Week,* none of which generated enough inquiries to justify their extremely high ad costs. On the assumption that Catholics concerned about the moral implications of their investments would likely also be conservative in their general outlook, we tried *National Review* (which was quite effective), *Weekly Standard* (which was a bust), and two conservative Catholic journals, *First Things* and *New Oxford Review* (both too small and specialized to be productive for us).

What may actually have been more effective than paid advertising, however, was publicity. We received excellent exposure in a wide range of general and business media. The idea of religiously-based investing seemed to tickle the fancy of business writers. But I learned something basic about the PR business through this experience — that public relations consultants generally have a limited number of good media contacts, and they tend to use them up quickly. We went through three different PR shops in that initial publicity effort. Each had success placing stories with a limited number of outlets. Then, the well would dry up, and we'd find ourselves hustling to generate fresh interest beyond those reporters with whom each agency was closely acquainted. Still, the effort paid off, and we got a significant amount of ink.

One of the most compelling "hooks" we had to interest news people was Tom Monaghan's involvement in the fund. Tom's personal story (spending part of his childhood in an orphanage, starting Domino's Pizza on a shoestring) had made him a particular favorite of writers who specialize in business stories with a human-interest slant. A 2001 profile in *Investor's Business Daily,* highlighting Tom's management style at Domino's Pizza, was a classic example of a whole genre of Monaghan reportage that continues to this day. The article noted how he "made managers jot down monthly reports about their jobs, outlining what they'd achieved and what their goals were for the next six months," and described how what *IBD* termed "the crusty ex-Marine" would then "sit with them for more than an hour going over what they wrote."

The main value of the "Tom" angle was that it put the face of a high-profile business figure on the story of Morally Responsible Investing, which I'm convinced benefited not only Ave Maria, but all the religiously themed funds that were around at the time. It helped to make this whole investment specialty hot news. We were covered by the Associated Press and the Dow Jones News Service, and got great exposure in business magazines and major papers around the country (overseas as well; one big hit was *Die Velt*, an important German newspaper). I even became something of a minor celebrity, myself, interviewed on radio and TV.[6]

The story was manna from heaven for clever headline writers who rolled out punchy lines like: "Religious Funds Help Investors Keep the Faith"; "In Mutual Funds We Trust"; "Seek and Ye Shall Find a Fund"; "Money Manager Makes a Hail Mary Play"; "Ave Maria Sings to Catholic Investors"; and endless variations. I have no doubt that we provided many of these scribes with their best opportunity to explore

---

6   This unaccustomed personal visibility got me invited to the White House to serve on the reception committee for Pope Benedict during his 2008 U.S. visit. What a kick! When the invitation arrived, I imagined Judi and me hanging out in the Oval Office with the Pope and President George W. Bush.

The first hint that my fantasies were slightly too elevated came after we submitted the information required for our security clearances. We received a follow-up email advising us that we had passed the background check, and suggesting we show up at the White House gate at least three hours in advance of the program. When Judi and I arrived on the big day, we understood why. The reception committee consisted of 10,000 people, all of whom were standing in a line that ran for about a mile around the presidential mansion.

We ended up rather far from the Pope and the President. Judi discovered a small knoll from which to glimpse the distant proceedings, and I stood under some trees on the far edge of the White House lawn. As things turned out, I found myself next to Fr. Frank Pavone, National Director of Priests for Life and the leading pro-life advocate in the country (maybe in the world). Fr. Frank and I had met before, but this gave us a chance to chat for an extended time. We discovered we shared a mutual friend, Fr. Douglas Mosey, president and rector of Holy Apostle Seminary in Cromwell, Connecticut. Fr. Douglas and I had been classmates at Detroit's Catholic Central High School.

The Pope finally did show and made some brief, inspirational remarks calling upon us to dedicate ourselves to protecting the sanctity of life. During his blessing of the crowd, I held up my rosary, which had previously been blessed by Pope John Paul II. I think that rosary is rather special, bearing the blessings of two popes. I carry it with me wherever I go.

religious phraseology since Sunday school days. But nothing can top the headline that appeared in *Mutual Fund News*, quoting CNBC's Maria Bartiromo, who began an interview by identifying my associate, Gregg Watkins, as manager of the "Oye Vey Maria! Fund."

Well, we took our exposure as we got it. In all, between advertising and PR expenses, the roll-out cost my company more than a million dollars. But where it worked, it worked well. We became a modest but recognized presence on the business-news scene.

The Bowie Factor

While we were gaining all this exposure, I invested countless hours calling on prospective investors. Many of these visits were made in the company of Bowie Kuhn. Having been involved in numerous Catholic causes over the years, Bowie had contacts in dioceses, schools, charitable organizations, and religious institutes all over the country, plus a Rolodex crammed with personal and business acquaintances. His connections and his boundless enthusiasm for the Morally Responsible Investing concept opened many doors, especially among Church hierarchy. Several bishops and cardinals were close friends, and even those who weren't held him in high regard.

Bowie once made an appointment with a cardinal to personally pitch the Ave Maria Mutual Funds for the archdiocesan investment portfolio. On the day of the scheduled presentation, Bowie called me to say he couldn't make the appointment due to a family emergency. I changed my schedule, making my way lickity-split to the site of that planned meeting. The cardinal walked into the room expecting to see Bowie, but instead found only me. "Glad to see you, George," he said politely, though with obvious disappointment, "but you're not Bowie Kuhn." (I had met him once before, and I was surprised he remembered me.) When the cardinal heard about Bowie's emergency, he very graciously spent 45 minutes with me. His Eminence expressed great concern, showing his respect and admiration for Bowie, whom he had never met.

Bowie had an undeniable cachet. He was well known, well liked, and recognized both in and out of the sports world, even long after he had retired from baseball. I remember walking down 42nd Street in New York with Bowie and his wife, Luisa. People would wave and call out, "How ya doin', Commish! What do you think of the Yankees' chances this year?" (and by then, he hadn't been Baseball Commissioner for over 20 years). Bowie was always generous with his time. He'd stop and talk to strangers, give autographs, discuss baseball. He had a photographic memory capable of recalling games, and even specific plays, that had occurred 30 or 40 years before.

I began to sense Bowie's unique value to our project very early in the development phase. In 2001, I mentioned to some friends that Bowie Kuhn would be participating in a strategy session for this new mutual fund I was planning, and they asked if they might stop by and meet him. "Sure," I said, thinking nothing of it. The next thing I knew, I was getting calls from friends, clients, family members, professional colleagues — every manner of acquaintance — asking: "Can I drop by? Mind if I bring the wife and kids?" We finally had to arrange for a large meeting room at the Birmingham Athletic Club, about a mile from my office, and served coffee and doughnuts to a crowd of over 100 people. It proved to be an unexpected kick start for the Ave Maria Catholic Values Fund. One attendee wrote a check for $300,000 on the spot, becoming one of our earliest large shareholders.

Bowie's personal appeal also reached deeply into the realm of media. I remember a particular occasion when I was to be interviewed by *The Wall Street Journal.* It was one of those loose, *next-time-you're-in-town* arrangements with a staff writer of decidedly junior status. The next time I *was* in town, I phoned to see if it would be convenient for him to do the interview, casually mentioning that Bowie Kuhn had made the trip to New York with me.

We set a meeting time, and when Bowie and I showed up, we found ourselves facing not only the young writer, but one of his senior staff colleagues, plus an editor. They were eager to quiz Bowie about the current state of Major League Baseball, that season's prospects for the Yankees, and other sports-business topics. He regaled them with his repertoire of fascinating baseball tales, including the fabled saga of his 1974 clash with Yankees owner, George

Steinbrenner. But along the way, the Ave Maria Mutual Funds got mentioned, and the result was some very nice publicity.

The Bowie magic was an asset in dealing with religious media as well. "The World Over — Live," EWTN's public affairs program, hosted by Raymond Arroyo (network news director), had long been at the top of my Catholic media hit list. Numerous calls to the show's producer always drew the same response: the interview schedule was full. I mentioned my frustration to Tom Monaghan, who suggested I offer Bowie for a joint interview. Bowie said he'd be happy to help, I called EWTN once more, and a week later the two of us were in the network's studio in Birmingham, Alabama.

We got an entire hour of air time, the first half of which was devoted to Bowie, his baseball adventures, and his involvements in assorted Catholic good works.[7] The second half focused on Morally Responsible Investing, with Bowie doing most of the talking, even about the Ave Maria Mutual Funds. My function in the discussion was mainly to answer viewer call-in questions about investing. But we gained terrific exposure to the EWTN audience, about 2.3 million at the time. Arroyo even had our toll-free phone number (866-AVE MARIA) superimposed on the screen. It turned out to be one of the most productive media contacts we ever made.

While Bowie would have been the first to admit he wasn't an investment expert, he understood the basic principles of investing. More importantly, he understood and had a great sensitivity to people — all kinds of people. In fact, it was his direct influence that brought Larry Kudlow to our Catholic Advisory Board. I had approached Larry originally, and he declined, wishing us well in our endeavor, but insisting that he had too many board and committee commitments already. I wasn't willing to give up, since I knew that having someone of Larry Kudlow's reputation and visibility on our board would give us the heft we needed. So I called Bowie Kuhn into action.

7　Bowie was especially avid in his support for Tom Monaghan's various endeavors, including Ave Maria University, Ave Maria School of Law, Legatus, and the Thomas More Law Center. He even served on the board of Tom's Ave Maria Foundation.

I made an arrangement for us to see Larry at his office, and Bowie did his magic. He talked about our mission, the importance of the work we had undertaken, how we were trying to offer Catholics an opportunity to invest in a manner consistent with their faith. Larry, a convert to Catholicism and strongly pro-life, identified with all that. Bowie proceeded to point out how our long-term goal was to change the culture by influencing Corporate America to stop supporting abortion. I began to notice that Larry was listening to what Bowie was telling him with a level of absorption I had never elicited in my previous attempts to make him understand our project.

Bowie turned Larry around completely. He did it quietly and persuasively by making Larry see that helping us wouldn't be a burden, but rather an opportunity to advance an important moral initiative. It was a masterful stroke of salesmanship — and I mean salesmanship in the most positive and constructive sense. Bowie was a good salesman because he believed in his cause, and so was able to speak from the heart. Once more it had its effect; Larry Kudlow joined our board on the spot.

Beside the circles of media, sports and Church, Bowie's contacts also extended deeply into the corporate world. He knew executives by the dozen — which proved extremely useful in cultivating relationships for many purposes. Bowie would phone CEOs of large corporations, asking that they accommodate my analysts with interviews and information as part of our investment research process. This was especially effective if the CEOs happened to be Catholic. But even if they weren't, the Bowie Kuhn name carried a lot of weight.

With his help, by the end of that first year, the Ave Maria Catholic Values Fund had more than 3,000 shareholders.

The Board Changes

Bowie's death in March 2007 was a real loss to us, as it was to the many Catholic institutions and apostolates to which he'd lent his support over the years. Not only had Bowie been a tireless proponent of Morally Responsible Investing, he had served as chairman of our Catholic Advisory Board, and his was one of the most visible faces associated with our enterprise. Indeed, Bowie's association with the Ave Maria Mutual Funds provided a critical element of credibility. Finding a successor was urgent; finding the *right* successor was crucial.

Since Bowie had been primarily identified with baseball, the question arose as to whether we should seek out another sports figure. The board members were attracted to the idea. But they determined that, whatever secular associations Bowie's successor might have, being a strong, committed Catholic was the first qualification. Several individuals were suggested, many competent and qualified, each with their plusses and minuses. When the name, Lou Holtz, was suggested, the board paused en mass.

This was a very provocative possibility. Lou had been head football coach at the University of Notre Dame, the absolute top-of-mind Catholic school in the country. He'd led the Fighting Irish to 23 consecutive victories over a two-year period, and won the national championship in 1988 (in only his second year as head coach). During earlier career years, he'd led six different teams to bowl games. And his personal recognition extended beyond the sports world. Aside from being one of the winningest coaches in NCAA history, he was known as a tremendous motivational speaker. Most important, he was strongly devoted to the Catholic Church, loyal to the Magisterium, and a deeply committed pro-life activist. The board agreed unanimously to ask him to join. With all his accomplishments, Lou Holtz is a very humble guy. His first reaction to our invitation was to tell me he felt inadequate for the post. "There's no way I can fill the shoes of the great Bowie Kuhn," he said. "But I'll just do the best I can to help you fellas with this important work." And so he has — marvelously.[8]

8   In mid 2009, I had the opportunity (and privilege) to introduce Coach Holtz at the Pershing Insite Investment Conference, where he was the keynote speaker. He talked to 1,000 financial advisors on how to live life and "be a champion every day." Coach is an outstanding orator and is highly sought as a motivational and inspirational speaker. Besides being a great college football coach and ESPN football analyst, he is a great human being. He's a leader, a teacher and a philosopher. His philosophy on life is geared toward hard work, discipline (particularly *self*-discipline), as well as self-reliance, good judgment, proper attitude, and everyday common sense. Coach is a real Catholic gentleman — role model — and I'm proud to have him on our Catholic Advisory Board.

chapter 3

A Lifetime Preparing

It goes without saying that I hope the people who read this book will grasp the importance of the MRI concept. And naturally, I hope some of those will consider the Ave Maria Mutual Funds as appropriate vehicles for investing. So I accept that it would be entirely fair to ask what it is that makes *me* the primary spokesman for Morally Responsible Investing — and for that matter, what qualities I bring to the management of the Ave Maria Funds. Accordingly, some personal reflection is in order.

Once I had gotten over my perplexity at the idea, proposed by Tom Monaghan and Bowie Kuhn, of starting a Catholic mutual fund (and especially, once I had come to the thought that such a thing might actually work), it occurred to me that I had been preparing for this endeavor my entire life. I mean that in more than the professional sense, having started my career with the venerable Detroit investment house, William C. Roney & Company, whose principal was a devout Catholic of high moral convictions and unimpeachable business ethics. Indeed, there were signs in my teen years — even my early childhood — which might have suggested this turn my career would take.

Born into a family with strong entrepreneurial instincts, I spent my elementary years in Detroit's Precious Blood School, run by the Adrian Dominican Sisters. It amazes me to see how this order has changed. Nowadays, the Adrian Dominicans are very much taken up with feminism, peace studies, and nature spirituality, but "back in the day," these sisters were known for being super-strict disciplinarians.[1] I recall a classmate, Ted Holloway, who considered Precious Blood more regimented than the private military school from which he had transferred. My own experience tended to confirm his impression.

Located in a largely blue-collar neighborhood in northwest Detroit, Precious Blood cost a family $20 a year for the first child attending; additional siblings were free. In the case of my own family, that meant my three brothers and I all attended at an average yearly tuition of $5.00, an unimaginable educational bargain today. But this was the 1950s, when parochial schools were staffed almost entirely by nuns, who worked for no pay, and the supply of habited teachers seemed virtually limitless.

Low cost and the Sisters' zeal for teaching the Faith in a straightforward and dependable manner guaranteed full classrooms, which averaged 64 students and made discipline a top priority. Looking back, the quickness of a nun with her trusty ruler — that staple of so many Catholic jokes and reminiscences — makes complete sense. It was a matter of fending off utter chaos. But these strict Sisters accomplished much. They taught us the Golden Rule, made vividly clear the difference between appropriate and inappropriate behavior, and impressed upon us the importance of trying to imitate Jesus and the Blessed Mother. Likewise, having the crucifix in every classroom provided a constant reminder that Christ died even for the sins of a bunch of rowdy, working-class kids.[2]

It all had its effect, which became especially clear to me at our 50th class reunion, held September 13, 2008. Fifty-two members of the

---

1   It's always a big deal in the diocesan paper when the Adrian Dominicans get a new vocation. But then, that's a situation faced by many religious communities that have cast off old characteristics and refashioned themselves along more "progressive" lines.

2   The devices which nuns employed to keep classroom life orderly were sometimes impenetrable to our young minds — for instance, the labeling of desks with pupils' initials to make sure each of us always sat in the right place. The desk of a classmate named Irene Stuecken bore the enigmatic label, "IS," prompting another pupil, Ricky Slaven, to ponder, in a sort of pre-Bill Clinton way, exactly what the meaning of "IS" is.

eighth-grade class of 1958 showed up, some coming from as far away as California, Florida, Texas and Washington. They shared their personal stories, and it was inspiring to hear how many still practiced the Faith and had passed it on to their kids and grandchildren. Their reflections put me in mind of some high-profile Catholic media figures, such as the late Tim Russert (who attended Catholic school in Buffalo) and Bill O'Reilly (who received his Catholic education on New York's Long Island), who have spoken with fondness and respect for the nuns who helped to form them as men.[3]

Indeed, the power of Catholic education in the 1950s is clearly evident to me. At least it is now. I must admit that my attitude at the time was something other than enthusiasm. Actually, I was terrified of the nuns, though fear never seemed to keep me from the rascally ways that regularly brought me under the wilting gaze of those formidable women. But somehow their lessons about doctrine and morals and ambition seeped into my troublemaking, pre-adolescent brain — especially ambition.

I was never particularly good at sports. Aside from a less-than-dazzling attempt at high school track, I channeled all my energies into those pursuits in which I thought I had a reasonable chance of excelling, such as band, serving at the altar, or being a safety crossing guard. One area in which I discovered a talent and the determination to succeed was salesmanship. I became a mainstay of the school fundraising program, selling copious quantities of raffle tickets, Christmas cards, and religious articles — in the process developing a high degree of personal discipline. I received encouragement in these efforts from my parents who, I suspect, saw the positive effects in building self-reliance.

Cultivating Character

My folks were big on self-reliance, especially my mother, Marian Schwartz, who was a strong woman much focused on cultivating char-

---

3   In his autobiography, *Pizza Tiger*, Tom Monaghan reflects lovingly on Sr. Beradra, who had a profound influence on him during his formative years in St. Joseph's Home for Boys, a Jackson, Michigan, orphanage run by the Felician nuns.

acter in her five children: my three older brothers — Walter, Bill and Greg — me, and my little sister, Marianne.

Mom stressed that character showed in a crisis, but you had to work at developing it so you'd have it when it counted. "Always do what you say you're going to do," was one of her favorite pieces of advice. She maintained that too many people over-promise and under-perform. Far better to under-promise and then perform beyond expectations.

It was a bit of wisdom which has stuck with me, and I've seen its truth demonstrated again and again in my investment practice. If I project a return for my clients of 10 to 12 percent, a 13-percent return is greeted as a windfall. On the other hand, if I indicate that 15 percent is the goal, but only hit 13, the very same 13 percent that would otherwise make me a hero is viewed with disappointment.

My dad, Walter Schwartz, provided me with our family's practical perspective on the work-a-day world. He was a lifelong businessman and heir to the American immigrant story. His father, Paul, had arrived in America in 1909 (at age 19), after a condiment-making business he'd operated in Germany with his brother and father was somehow judged a critical national asset and taken over by the Kaiser's government. "Opa," as he would later be known to his grandchildren, was introduced to American free enterprise working in a German-language tavern, where his pay was $2.00 a week and "all the food I could steal." With classic immigrant pluck, Opa capitalized on his skill at making mustard and vinegar, building a new condiments business, which he eventually sold to the Great Atlantic & Pacific Tea Company (A&P), one of the pioneers of American supermarkets.[4]

---

4   Opa never forgot the workman's skills that were the basis of his business success. He would brag to his grandchildren about how he could roll a wooden barrel filled with 300 pounds of mustard across the room, making it go anywhere he wanted, all with one finger. At the outbreak of World War I, he received a friendly greeting from the Kaiser, urging him to come home and defend the "Vaterland," to which he replied with the German equivalent of, "Yeah, right!"

My grandmother's story illustrates another aspect of the immigrant experience. She too had come to America as a teenager, but in the capacity of something rather like an indentured servant. Anna — or "Oma," as we called her — worked as an upstairs maid for a Jewish doctor in New Jersey. The memory of those days gave her a deep appreciation for hard, menial work and those who did it. She and Opa met at a German social club, and the rest is family history.

Steeped in that tradition of boot-strap initiative, my father made his mark in Detroit's machine-tools industry. He always counseled me to "do something you like," observing that, "you'll probably be good at it, and you'll make a good living." While my youthful dreams inclined me to crave more than just a "good living" (I wanted to make a GREAT living), the wisdom of his advice has been borne out. I've been fortunate to spend my adult life doing work I enjoy, and I've made quite a nice living. I've learned something about self-reliance in the process: It's better to *earn* money than to win it, inherit it, or have it given to you. A thousand dollars gained through your own effort brings more genuine satisfaction than ten thousand you fall into.

Both of my parents were great education advocates, and when my days at Precious Blood were over, they sent me to another superb Catholic school, Detroit Catholic Central High School. Run by the Basilian Fathers, Catholic Central was known for the motto, "Teach me goodness, discipline and knowledge." The Basilians took that motto seriously — not only the words, but the order of priorities. Morality was first on their agenda, and they were no shrinking violets in promoting it. Discipline was the primary method of instruction, right up to corporal punishment. But I'm convinced that their toughness was based in love. To this day I remain in awe of these fine and dedicated men, and in fact, I now serve on the Catholic Central High School Board of Trustees. I consider it a great privilege.

My parents were pro-life in the way most Catholics in the 1950s and early 1960s were pro-life — which is to say the casual and widespread acceptance of abortion would have been unthinkable to them. Likewise, they readily perceived the harmful effects of pornography and other sources of unwholesome influence. This was the common Christian understanding of the day, and it provided the fertile soil in which conscience could take root.

But it was the Basilian Fathers of Catholic Central who first opened my eyes to the specific evils of abortion. I think my teachers could see the moral revolution that was looming on the horizon. They made us face the horrors of a society willing to kill its babies — often taking flack from people who didn't want to think about such things

— and it was their candor and courage that set me on the path toward my later-life emergence into the activism of Morally Responsible Investing.

I am grateful that neither my parents nor I ever considered any sort of education appropriate for me other than Catholic education — which continued through the Jesuit-founded University of Detroit. Not that a Jesuit school was without its quirks. By the mid-1960s, the Society of Jesus was well on its way to gaining its current baleful reputation as a leftist debating club.

I recall one professor (a layman, as it happened, but very much under Jesuit influence) who spent much time praising the virtues of labor unions. With my mother's help, I crafted an essay critiquing compulsory unionization, arguing how, in the name of protecting workers from the depredations of evil, profit-mongering companies, unions crippled imagination and stifled initiative. The instructor returned my paper with a note calling the essay "a great diatribe" and speculating that I must come from a family of "union busters."[5] But, he also gave me an A-minus, which, considering his labor sympathies, I took as a compliment and a statement of his integrity as a teacher.

---

5   I will confess to a less-than-sympathetic attitude toward unionization which dates from an internship I had one summer during college at the Dodge Truck Assembly plant in Warren, Michigan. Starting out by unloading truck parts from freight cars, I was promoted to operating a forklift (called a "hi-low" in those days), and discovered I was skilled at moving a lot of material quickly. The union operators resented a non-union college kid doing their job so efficiently, and complained that I was making them look bad. I dismissed their criticism until one incident provided me with an insight into the "union mentality" underlying their annoyance with my speed; it has stuck with me all my life.

A container had fallen off one of the hi-lows (driven by a union operator), strewing millions of tiny machine screws all over the floor and virtually shutting down a full day's production. I and several of my fellow interns were recruited to clean up the mess, since the union operators refused to do anything other than drive their lifts. "Work rules," they insisted. And therein lies the fundamental problem at the heart of the auto industry's woes, a problem which no amount of government bailouts will ever touch.

Unions undoubtedly played their part in lifting workers from the depths of exploitation, and helped build the great American middle class. But I'm convinced that the labor movement has had its day. There are ways to protect the rights of workers without crippling the industries on which their jobs depend.

Such was the atmosphere of learning created by the Jesuits, who even in their present state of confusion, are still recognized as champions of Catholic education.

And so the influence of my parents, the Adrian Dominicans, the Basilian Fathers, and even the Jesuits combined to shape me into a person for whom conscience and commitment have meaning and importance. My outlook was evident early, as one incident from teen years illustrates. Driving on icy streets, I was rammed at an intersection by a driver who, it turned out, had a police record with numerous traffic violations (and worse). I was summoned to testify about the incident some seven months in the future. When I showed up at court on the appointed date, I was met by a startled prosecutor who told me there had been a plea agreement in the case.

"I didn't call you to reconfirm that you should be here," he said. "We always call the witnesses to tell them they're needed. Nobody ever shows up unless they're called."

I just shrugged. "Well, you had sent me a summons," I explained. "I marked it on my calendar, and here I am. You didn't have to call me. It's my civic duty to be here."

He was quite stunned.

I hope it does not exceed the limits of modesty to say that I continue to live by this understanding of personal obligation. In fact, my annoyance with the practice of reminder calls — whether about pending medical appointments or having my cleaning picked up — makes me something of a pain to those who no doubt consider it a service of convenience. In my mind, people should simply do what they have set themselves to do.

Some years ago, a young man in my neighborhood discovered just how prickly I can be on that subject. I had paid the fellow in advance to put up a Christmas light display on my house — a job he abandoned in the middle, leaving its completion to me. When he called some weeks later to ask if he could earn another fee by removing the lights, he met with my disdain.

"You've got to be kidding," I said. "You didn't fulfill your commitment to put the lights up. Why should I pay you to take them down?"

He was outraged, believing that I was somehow cheating him.

"Young man," I said, "I'm going to teach you something that — if you listen carefully and live by it — will serve you the rest of your life. *Do what you say you're going to do, regardless of what it costs you, regardless of how much pain and discomfort you must endure.* You have shown a lack of character by not following through on your commitment. I suggest you work on developing that character. It will make you a happier and more prosperous person."

I have often wondered if he took my words to heart. And I guess I'll always have to wonder, because I won't hire him again. I do know that living up to commitments has served me well from the earliest days of working, which for me began with a *Detroit News* paper route at age eight (actually half of my brother, Gregory's, 64-customer route — an unofficial arrangement, since paperboys were required to be at least 12). I handled the job well for two years, until I was ten. Then I got sick, and in what one might call an "unfriendly takeover," my mother sold the route on me. With my duties as an altar boy and crossing guard, along with playing in the school band, she worried that I was over-committed and becoming over-stressed.

Enterprise, Thrift and Faith

My first encounter with the risks and rewards of entrepreneurship came at nine years old, shoveling snow for a neighbor, Mr. Rosenbaum, for $1.00. He was impressed with my work, and offered me a contract to keep his driveway clear for the remainder of the winter. His proposal was simple: "I'll give you $10 now, if you come back and shovel every time it snows, no matter how much or how little snow we get."

The risk to me was extra work at no more pay. But the upside possibility was intriguing. I calculated that we probably wouldn't get ten more snowfalls that winter, so I was likely to at least make my $1.00 fee for each shoveling. And if the season proved especially mild, I could come out markedly ahead. I took the deal and won — snow was light that year. This was an important lesson about the moral rightness of a fair exchange. Both Mr. Rosenbaum and I had taken a risk, but in so doing, we each gained what we needed. He was guaranteed a clean driveway, and I made money.

My entrepreneurial appetite whetted, I launched on a series of childhood ventures. I learned the importance of drawing attention to good service by cutting the lawn of our highly visible corner home. My dad paid me $4.00, since our yard was larger than most on our block.[6] I offered the same service to my neighbors — who could see how well manicured I kept our lawn, and whose own yards were smaller — for only $2.00, which they perceived as a bargain.

I was caddying at the Detroit Golf Club at 11 (as with my *Detroit News* paper route, beginning under the usual minimum age of 12; I convinced the caddy master I could handle the job), earning $3.25 per round, plus tips. On a good day I could do the course twice. It's a testament to the contrast between the world of my childhood and the world of today that my mother urged me to hitchhike the four miles between the club and home in order to save the $.20 a day it cost for the bus (which she referred to with the quaint, *Brooklynesque* expression, "carfare"). What parent would consider such a practice safe in our current moral climate?

At 17, I had a summer job in a local bottling factory, earning $1.77 per hour stacking cases of Hires Root Beer and Squirt. The next summer I drove a Pepperidge Farm bread truck, delivering to grocery stores around Detroit. That was followed by my summer at the Dodge Truck assembly plant — 90 days only; if I'd worked a day longer, I would have been required to join the UAW.

Not only was I an industrious youth, I was thrifty — another habit acquired from my mother, who was one of the all-time great bargain hunters. My brothers and I liked to take in Saturday matinees at the Mercury Theater, which was located next to Precious Blood School (and where, in 1952, the entire student body made a pilgrimage to see

---

6   Our backyard didn't receive the same close care as the front. My brothers and I played football in the back, with fearful consequences for the lawn. Once my father was asked why he permitted his sons to do such damage. His reply was a brilliant statement of fatherly love: "I'm raising kids, not grass."

"The Song of Bernadette"[7]). We immersed ourselves in Superman movies and the grade-B horror films so fondly remembered from the 1950s, like "The Blob," "The Thing," and "War of the Worlds," along with assorted westerns starring such notables as Roy Rogers, Gene Autry, and Lash LaRue ("King of the Bullwhip"), even the occasional old chestnut featuring Tom Mix. I would start the day with a quarter set aside from lawn mowing, snow shoveling, or caddying, pay the $.14 admission fee, lay out a nickel for a Coke and another nickel for popcorn, and emerge from an afternoon of cinematic fantasy with a penny left over — which I would then save. Our modern age of wall-to-wall media offers no entertainment value comparable to that.

I have found frugality an advantage in life. It retains great importance to me (as my wife and children can attest), especially in current circumstances when the ability to get by on a little less is becoming a priority. Indeed, those who see bargain hunting as a trial, or who equate extravagance with satisfaction (or worse, with personal fulfillment), grieve much in challenging times. I'm glad to have been spared such expectations.

But in all, I think the dominant characteristic derived from these experiences of youth is my Catholicity. The quest for piety and Christian virtue (though not always their attainment) has been a reality to me since my altar-boy days. How well I recall memorizing Latin prayers in order to give the appropriate responses during the old Tridentine liturgy (Monsignor Hermes had little patience with boys who forgot them or pronounced them wrong[8]); getting up in darkness on cold Detroit mornings to serve at 6:00 a.m. Mass (my father would have to drive me there on time, God bless him); kneeling on the hard marble sanctuary steps, as if in personal penance, and reciting the

---

7   Released in 1943, "The Song of Bernadette" stared Jennifer Jones in an Academy Award-winning performance as Bernadette Soubirous, the French peasant girl who experienced apparitions of the Virgin Mary in 1858. Directed by Henry King, the film was a production of 20th Century Fox.

8   Monsignor Hermes, our pastor, was not only something of a taskmaster to the altar boys, he was scrupulously careful in his celebration of Mass, taking a full hour every time. I much preferred serving for Fr. McNichols, the associate, who could get through a weekday Mass in 15 minutes flat, including distribution of Communion.

Confiteor (*Mea culpa, mea culpa, mea maxima culpa* — "Through my fault, through my fault, through my most grievous fault").

Challenges of Life

The nuns and priests who taught me were demanding — in some cases, perhaps, overly so — but my schooling gave me a foundation of faith and prepared me for some challenges that would prove pivotal. The first occurred at age 17, during a picnic the day after my senior prom. Despite my athletic deficiencies, I foolishly chose to play touch football with members of the varsity football team. I slipped on some gravel, came down sideways on my right leg, and snapped both bones (tibia and fibula) below the knee — double compound fractures, with chunks of bone actually coming out through the skin. I was laid up with my leg in a cast for nine months. It proved to be a remarkable time of growth, during which time my mother taught me much about the power of prayer.

Seven years later, I would be involved in the crash of a six-passenger Piper Cherokee, en route to northern Michigan with my father, my brother, Greg, and Dad's friend, Andy Farkas (a former Washington Redskins all-pro football player). We were to inspect some property which the pilot, a real estate agent, was representing, when we ran into a snow storm and lost visibility. Lacking a rating to fly on instruments, our pilot/salesman was unable to find the airport. We ran out of gas and went down in the north woods. As we lay in the rubble waiting for help, me with my back broken in five places, I realized the extent of my father's faith and courage. He kept repeating, "Hang in there, George. God loves us. He'll look after us." This from a man who was enduring two ankles severely mangled, one nearly severed.

I spent a year recuperating, encouraged by my mother's words — "Whatever doesn't kill you makes you stronger"[9] — and experiencing

---

9   I doubt she realized it, but my mother was actually paraphrasing Friedrich Nietzsche ("That which does not kill us makes us stronger"). The 19th-Century German philosopher was a man of profoundly antireligious sentiments with whom my mother would have agreed about very little.

the redemptive force of suffering. I learned much about what the body can endure, about patience, and about the true source of healing. In the process, I discovered strengths I might otherwise never have come to know, strengths which were, in the most literal sense, *given* to me, and which would prove to be my sustenance throughout numerous trials and setbacks in my business life.

That life has been spent in investments, a world which might seem a most unspiritual realm of professional concern. But then, what is it that I have been doing these 40-plus years? My career has focused on the analysis of potential earning opportunities and on advising people as to whether those opportunities are valid and applicable to their financial goals. To put it another way, I have helped people secure their futures and protect themselves and their families against the vicissitudes of life. And that, it seems to me, is a Christian service.

My professional résumé is quite simple, but the experience it suggests is deep. I received my degree in finance from the University of Detroit in 1966. Between 1967 and 1974, I served as an investment research analyst with two New York Stock Exchange member firms in Detroit: William C. Roney & Company; and Manley, Bennett, McDonald & Co. I then became senior investment officer and chairman of the investment committee at the National Bank & Trust Company of Ann Arbor, Michigan. I founded my own firm, Schwartz Investment Counsel, Inc.[10], in 1980, and launched the Schwartz Value Fund in 1984. I am a Chartered Financial Analyst charterholder, a Chartered Investment Counselor, and an active member of several investment professional organizations.

This is a summary of my personal history — the events of which have brought me to my current involvement with Morally Responsible Investing and the Ave Maria Mutual Funds. I would never have predicted such an outcome at the start of my career. But looking back at the progression, I can discern a certain logic, even the Hand of Providence, directing my journey. In any event, I cannot express how

---

10 Additional information about my professional practice and range of services offered by Schwartz Investment Counsel, Inc. is available online at: http://www.schwartzinvest.com.

deeply gratified I feel that my professional expertise has made it possible for me to advance a distinctly moral effort, to serve the Church, and in a very real way, to help spread the Faith.

Personal observation and a wide range of studies confirm that America is a faithful country — far more so than the "Christian" nations of Europe, most of which have reached a decidedly post-Christian stage in their cultural lives (Europe is approaching cultural transformation; many countries could become predominantly Muslim in a generation or so). Some 90 percent of Americans routinely tell pollsters that faith is important to them; more than 80 percent specifically declare themselves Christians, whether or not they attend church. Even so secular a source as the American Association of Retired Persons reports that 80 percent of respondents to a survey conducted by the association's magazine reported they believe in miracles.[11]

While the moral picture of modern American society has become somewhat, shall we say, "clouded," the USA is a country that still accepts the idea that there are distinctions between right and wrong. This gives me enormous hope for the potential impact of Morally Responsible Investing as a lever of ethical change. I am truly honored to champion this cause.

---

11 In its issue for January and February 2009 *AARP The Magazine* (which claims the largest circulation of any periodical in the world) reported on a survey of 1,300 Americans age 45 and older, in which not only 80 percent of respondents said they believe in miracles, but 41 percent said they think miracles happen every day, and 37 percent claimed to have witnessed a miracle. The survey also found that most people are convinced miracles are supernatural in origin, with 84 percent of those attributing miracles to God, and some 75 percent specifically to either Jesus or the Holy Spirit. Even allowing for the survey's skew toward older adults, these results underscore America's religious character.

Family Circle (circa 1948) — The cradle of both my Catholicism and my entrepreneurial outlook, our household was typical of Catholic families in the early 1950s, steeped in the values of traditional Christianity and American free enterprise. My parents taught my brothers and me to be honest and hard-working, and always to deliver on our promises. From left, back row, my brothers Bill, Walter Jr., and Greg; front row, my father, Walter, me at age 4, my mother, Marian. (My sister, Marianne, would come along in 1949.) It was a real "Ozzie and Harriet" upbringing, though despite Mom's resemblance to the mild-mannered Harriet Nelson, she was the resident disciplinarian.

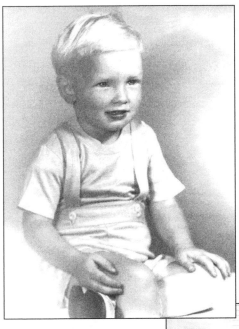

First Portrait —
A two-year-old me.

Ride 'em, Cowboy —
My three brothers and I were avid fans of the western heroes so beloved in the 1950s, eagerly following their adventures during Saturday matinees at Detroit's Mercury Theater. At age 5, I got the chance to indulge my cowboy fantasies when a fellow came to our neighborhood offering pony rides. Looking back, it occurs to me that the pony-ride man was likely one of the first entrepreneurs with whom I came into contact outside my own family.

Finding My Strengths — While I was always a sports enthusiast, my experiences on the Catholic Central High School track team pretty much convinced me that athletics were not my strong suit. My appearance in the yearbook team photo (above, front row, fifth from right) documents my brief career as a runner, but I clocked better results as a clarinetist in the marching band (below, front row, fourth from left). Still, my absolute best accomplishments came when I was involved in school fundraisers. I discovered a flair for salesmanship which has proven a great benefit throughout my career.

The Way We Were — My 1966 college yearbook portrait records a youthful George Schwartz who today exists only in my mind's eye. But I really did look so fresh and clean-scrubbed once upon a time. Likewise, I recall fondly a perky, young Judith Pearl Arnold — "the smartest girl at Immaculata High School" — who would become my "pearl of great value."

Memory Lane — Me on a recent visit to my Detroit boyhood home. The old place still retains its charm, and lots of good memories of my early business venture, cutting lawns.

Alma Maters — My years at Detroit's Catholic Central High School were highly formative. The Basilian Fathers who ran the school opened my eyes to the truth about abortion. I'm proud to serve on the board of Catholic Central today. However, my formal Catholic education began in Precious Blood Parish (below), where I attended the local elementary school, now closed. Precious Blood is still an active parish, though under a different name, St. Peter Claver Parish.

Then and Now — Judi and me in October 1967, as we embarked on our life together (top); and the two of us as we are now, not quite as youthful as back in the day.

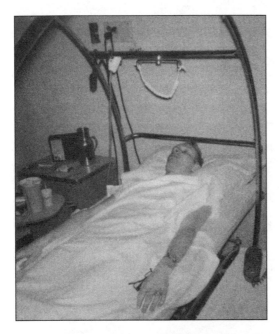

A Challenging Ordeal — An ill-fated flight through a northern Michigan storm left the small plane I was flying in a mangled mess (below) and me with multiple spinal fractures. For months I lay bound to a Stryker Circle Bed that could flip over to change my position. The experience taught me about what the human body can endure.

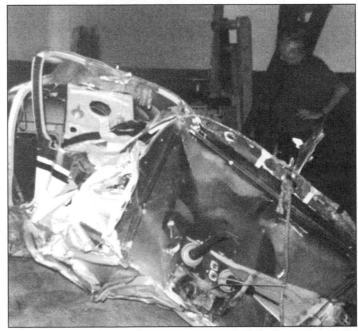

Immigrant Roots — My family traces its entrepreneurial tradition to my grandparents, Paul and Anna Schwartz, who came to the U.S. from Germany in the early years of the 20th century. Opa's skill at making condiments launched us on our pursuit of the American Dream, while Oma's experience as a domestic servant instilled an essential respect for hard work, which has carried down through the generations. (Photo circa 1945.)

Family Milestone — My parents, Walter and Marian Schwartz, celebrated their 50th wedding anniversary in September 1986. Making it to the half-century mark is a real testament to the sanctity of marriage, a concept that's a factor in Morally Responsible Investing.

59

My Investing Mentor — While Warren Buffett is 180 degrees away from my views on a number of subjects (especially abortion), the "Oracle of Omaha" is unquestionably a master's master when it comes to investing, and his influence on my professional development has been profound.

One of Buffett's great assets in stock analysis is a prodigious memory. I had asked him a question from the floor during Berkshire Hathaway's 1982 annual meeting. At the next year's session I had another question, and was frantically waving my hand to be recognized. Buffett looked at me and said, "Mr. Schwartz, you'll have to be patient; I'll get to you." I was amazed that he'd remembered me from a brief question the year before.

My Team — The staff of Schwartz Investment Counsel, Inc., on the lawn outside of our distinctive Bloomfield Hills, Michigan, headquarters building.

Three Guys with an Idea — The Ave Maria Mutual Funds sprang from the fertile imaginations of three Catholic laymen with a reformist bent: from left, the late Bowie Kuhn, myself, and Tom Monaghan. Our collaboration proved to be effective. The funds now have more than 25,000 shareholders.

Super Salesman — The late Bowie Kuhn was passionately devoted to the concept of Morally Responsible Investing and the Ave Maria Mutual Funds in which that idea has found expression. He promoted them tirelessly at every available forum, such as on "Kresta in the Afternoon," the daily radio program of Catholic talk show host Al Kresta (right). The Kresta show is carried on about 120 Catholic radio stations as well as Sirius Satellite Radio.

Board Members — Our Catholic Advisory Board currently consists of (top row) Larry Kudlow, CNBC market analyst and commentator; Catholic scholar and author, Michael Novak; Paul Roney, CPA, Executive Director of The Ave Maria Foundation; (bottom row) author and activist, Phyllis Schlafly; former University of Notre Dame football coach, Lou Holtz; and entrepreneur/philanthropist, Tom Monaghan — who, along with the late Bowie Kuhn and myself, founded the Ave Maria Mutual Funds. Bowie was the board's first chairman. That duty is performed now by Paul Roney.

As at the launching of our first fund, the involvement of such distinguished Catholic laymen is essential in giving us credibility. Many shareholders have indicated that their confidence in us has been enhanced by the presence of these remarkable people who were willing to put their names and personal reputations behind the promise of Morally Responsible Investing.

Board Meeting — Members of the Ave Maria Mutual Funds' Catholic Advisory Board at a recent meeting: from left, Phyllis Schlafly; Michael Novak; Lou Holtz; Paul Roney; my colleagues, Tim Schwartz, CFA, and Greg Heilman, CFA, who work closely with the board; yours truly; and Tom Monaghan. Larry Kudlow was not present for the photo.

Phyllis Schlafly and I share a quick consultation at dinner, after a recent Catholic Advisory Board meeting. A true heroine of the pro-life movement, Phyllis has stamped her strong personality on many aspects of the nation's political life.

Symbol of Achievement — The Ave Maria Growth Fund received the 2009 Lipper Fund Award as number one among 653 funds in its category (Multi-Cap Core), largely due to the work of portfolio managers Chris Sydlowsky, CFA (left) and Jim Bashaw, Jr., CFA.

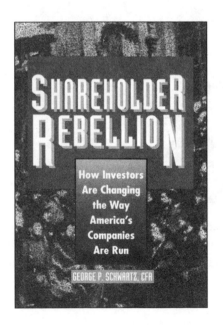

Earlier Book — My first foray into the world of literary expression was a book titled *Shareholder Rebellion*. Published in 1995, it reflected an activist tendency that would come to fruition in the idea of Morally Responsible Investing.

chapter 4

Money, Mind & Faith

It is an unfortunate truth — but a truth, nonetheless — that most investors don't make very much money in the stock market. The reason is simple, they buy high and sell low. Of course, they know they should be doing just the opposite. They understand that the idea is to buy a stock more cheaply than the price to which it can ultimately rise. Indeed, they would admit that it's foolish to do anything else.

Moreover, when I talk about Warren Buffett's *contrarian* practices or the principles of Value Investing, people have no trouble recognizing the simple truth in what I'm saying. Buffett's approach is so obvious: *Buy when everybody else is selling and driving the price down.* Likewise, Value Investing is no big mystery: *Do your homework, and go with a company that has good management, strong numbers, and sound business characteristics.* What could be more sensible?

Yet, most investors continue to do precisely the wrong thing. Why? Because they are human beings whose actions are driven by the *psychology* intrinsic to the human condition. Psychology may be the least appreciated aspect of investing. More often than not, people's investment behavior has less to do with the prospects of companies than with what those people assume, believe and feel about their own prospects. Their decision making reflects not so much reasoned choice as it does their confidence or anxiety, optimism or pessimism, the emotions and conflicts they're experiencing at a particular moment. So in large measure, the study of investing is about the study of investors.

Jason Zweig, a financial columnist for *The Wall Street Journal*, has delved deeply into the behavior and decision-making patterns of investors. In his book, *Your Money & Your Brain*,[1] he surveys research being conducted in an emerging field called *neuroeconomics* which seeks to discover how the human brain functions when confronted with choices about money. Zweig calls neuroeconomics a "science," though it's probably still a bit too new to bear that exalted title without challenge. At this point, the term "research specialty" would probably be most accurately descriptive. In any event, work under way in this field shows considerable promise in applying the techniques of neurobiological analysis to discerning why investors do the things they do.

Applied Technology

Neuroeconomic research is made possible by advances in the monitoring and imaging processes that have become indispensable in medical diagnostics. Scientists are able to observe brain activity in *real time* when test subjects are presented with different investment-related options and problems. They can track and record neural activity corresponding to the choices and reactions prompted by various situations confronting test participants. Some of the observations made in these exercises are quite revealing.

For instance, Zweig's book reports on studies conducted at Harvard Medical School by neuroscientist, Hans Breiter, in which magnetic resonance imaging was used to compare neural responses in the brains of cocaine addicts expecting a drug fix with those of other participants expecting to make money. Brieter found that the patterns of neurons firing in the two groups of images were "...virtually right on top of each other. You can't get a better bull's-eye hit than those two." The scientist believes that such an extremely close resemblance suggests there was more than simple anticipation at work in this exper-

---

1   *Your Money & Your Brain: How the New Science of Neuroeconomics Can Help Make You Rich*, by Jason Zweig, published by Simon & Schuster (2007).

iment. Rather, the expectation of reward may actually have something like "addictive" power. As Zweig explains it, "...once you score big on a few investments in a row, you may be the functional equivalent of an addict — except the substance you're hooked on isn't alcohol or cocaine, it's money."[2]

The apparent cause is release of dopamine, a brain chemical that, among other things helps us "...figure out how to take actions that will result in rewards at the right time." In Breiter's study, awareness of possible rewards to come caused the brains of both the addicts expecting their drugs and the test subjects expecting a monetary payoff to pump out dopamine. That created the pleasing "high" each group associated with what they wished to receive. From an investment point of view, this underscores the difficulty of keeping your cool and being able to make objective judgments, especially after you've experienced previous success. Because once you've felt the dopamine rush, you're inclined to want it again.

In contrast, Zweig recounts a study, in which he participated, designed to measure the effect of fear on decision making. The experiment involved a video card game in which participants chose between options that presented varying degrees of risk and monetary reward. Physical responses (breathing, heartbeat, perspiration, muscle activity) were monitored throughout the game. Zweig found himself increasingly making lower-risk card selections, even though accepting a higher degree of risk offered the prospect of making more money. Afterward he was surprised to discover that his recorded responses indicated levels of fear he would never have expected from such a game.

> "At first, the printout showed, my skin would sweat, my breath quicken, my heart race, my facial muscles furrow immediately after I clicked on any card that cost me money. Early on, when I drew one card that lost me $1,140, my pulse rate shot from 75 to 145 in a split second. After three or four bad losses from

2 *Your Money & Your Brain*, pages 66-67.

the risky decks, my bodily responses began surging before I selected a card from either of those piles. Merely moving the cursor over the riskier decks, without even clicking on them, was enough to make my physiological functions go haywire...."[3]

Such research indicates how reactions that exist well below the level of conscious awareness influence choices we assume are being made through reasoned assessment of options and outcomes. For all of our supposed intelligence and sophistication, we aren't separated from the primal responses that are essential to physical life. Fear is implanted in us. It is a gift from God, actually, intended to warn us when there is a possibility of danger. It has allowed our survival as a species. And we shouldn't be surprised that fear can become attached to concerns about money. As neuroscientist Antonio Damasio observes, "Money represents the means of maintaining life and sustaining us as organisms in our world."[4] So the possibility of its loss naturally makes us afraid.

Zweig says that the challenge investors face is learning to differentiate between *reflexive* judgment (responses that occur automatically on the neural/physical level) and *reflective* judgment (intentional, logical choice). He insists that we should never try to detach ourselves from the signals our brains are sending us — not that we ever really could. Rather, we should try to recognize those interior functions, rely on them to alert us when something seems wrong, then keep our heads and proceed sensibly.

Good advice, but easier said than done. The stock market meltdown of Fall 2008 and early 2009, arguably the most threatening economic event since the Great Depression, demonstrated the effect of fear on investor behavior. Typical reactions hardly reflected Warren Buffett's sanguine advice about how this was a great buying opportunity. Whether or not investors gave voice to the sentiment, their neu-

3   *Your Money & Your Brain*, page 164.
4   *Your Money & Your Brain*, page 165.

rons were shouting loud and clear; "That's all very good for Warren Buffett. *Sell!*"

At the height of the panic I heard from numerous clients dazed by the carnage, wondering which stocks to dump, or just seeking reassurance. One called with absolute terror in his voice. "Get me out of everything," he said. "Turn it into cash before it all falls apart."

I counseled patience. "The market will get through this and turn around," I said calmly. "Our funds are perfectly sound."

But he was having none of it. "Are they FDIC-insured?" he asked.

"No," I explained, "the FDIC only insures bank deposits."

"Then I'm cashing out. I can't take it anymore." With his sense of risk aversion raised to such a high level, there was nothing I could do to assuage his fear.

The answer to such panic is *common sense*, which as the old maxim reminds us, really isn't all that common. Webster's defines it as "practical judgment or intelligence; ordinary good sense," attributes we all like to believe we possess. But how quickly you can lose your grip on them when your expectations are suddenly upended. And it isn't only fear of loss that makes one behave irrationally. Anticipation of gain also plays havoc with your ability to see clearly and act sensibly.

Bubbles and Frenzies

Most investors have heard of the famous "Tulip Mania," a great speculative wave that swept the business community of Holland in the early 17th Century. Increased public interest in the flower, which had been introduced into Europe from the Ottoman Empire, sent prices of tulip bulbs soaring, setting off wild speculation in contracts to grow them (essentially, an early version of derivatives-futures trading). At the height of the frenzy in 1637, bulb contracts were said to sell for as much as 10 times a skilled craftsman's annual earnings. Naturally, such a run-up was unsustainable, and the market for tulip futures collapsed, with none of the contracts ever actually being fulfilled. The incident has since served as an object lesson about greed and how expectations can become inflated beyond rational judgment.

A century later, investors lost their lace-cuffed shirts over the infamous "South Sea Bubble." In this episode, Britain's South Sea Company gained trading concessions in the Americas in exchange for assuming government debt run up during the War of the Spanish Succession (1701-1714). Much of this trade — and there really was very little of it — involved transporting slaves from Africa. But excitement about vast wealth to be gained in the new world and a scheme whereby certain investors (mostly high-ranking British politicians) were guaranteed a buy-back of their shares fueled a speculative bubble that drove South Sea stock up ten-fold in a year.

This prompted the formation of other companies obliquely related to overseas trade, whose stock issues benefited from the frenzy. In one famous instance, a new company advertised that its activities were secret (eerily foreshadowing the 1990s boom in which investors had no idea what many of the dot-com companies did). By 1720, when the earliest South Sea subscribers were due a return on their investments, it became apparent that the great New World trader was not going to make good on its highly leveraged debt obligations. A general financial crisis ensued, forcing action by the government and the reorganization of the company. (Sound familiar?) Investors from virtually all strata of society learned a hard lesson about the emotion which Fed Chairman Alan Greenspan would later (in the 1990s) call, "irrational exuberance."[5] Isaac Newton, a firsthand observer of the bubble, commented, "I can calculate the movement of the stars, but not the madness of men."

Over the centuries, with depressing regularity, people have gotten swept up in the mania of the day — be it British railway speculation, the wild margin trading of the late 1920s (resulting in the crash of '29), or the '90s Internet bubble — buying without regard to value, and then later regretting their foolishness. Again and again, we've seen how otherwise reasonable, rational, intelligent human beings can lose their heads and their money.

---

5   Greenspan offered a perceptive observation that is very much to the point: "It is human psychology that drives a competitive market economy. And that process is inextricably linked to human nature, which appears essentially immutable and, thus, anchors the future to the past."

There's even a genre of books dealing with the subject, from Charles Mackay's *Extraordinary Popular Delusions and the Madness of Crowds*[6] (a classic whose title pretty much says it all), through *Manias, Panics and Crashes: A History of Financial Crises*, by Charles P. Kindleberger and Robert Z. Aliber.[7] These books (and others between and since) attempt to explain this durable aspect of human behavior.

Following the Herd

Why do people lose their minds in a crowd or in the excitement of a rapidly moving market? Part of the answer surely is simple conformism, the psychology of the "herd." Neuroeconomic research confirms the power of peer influence. Watching others adopt particular practices or try new things offers a certain emotional reassurance. They rationalize that if others are doing it, it must be safe to do. Under such influence, it doesn't matter all that much where the herd is going, as long as they keep moving with it. And so investors often behave like lemmings, those ugly little Norwegian rodents observed to fling themselves en mass into bodies of water.[8]

In recent years, another methodology for studying investing-related behavior has appeared on the academic scene. Known as *Behavioral Finance*, and based on a field of social science research called *heuristics*,[9] it's not unrelated to neuroeconomics, but it takes a somewhat different approach, exploring economic decision making from the perspective

---

6   Published in 1841, the book dealt with a variety of fads and frenzies, including witch hunting and alchemy. Its analysis of financial madness remains the book's most oft-cited contribution to the study of human psychology. Scotsman Charles Mackay was a journalist, a poet and the author of several popular songs. He gained international recognition through his coverage of the American Civil War for the *Times* of London.

7   Published by John Wiley & Sons, Inc. in 1978, and currently in its fifth edition.

8   Contrary to popular myth, lemmings don't commit group suicide prompted by mass hysteria. However, they do migrate in large colonies, often crossing lakes and rivers in the process, which is apparently the basis of this common misunderstanding.

9   The term *heuristics* refers to experience-based problem-solving techniques. Their study is extensively described in *Judgment under Uncertainty: Heuristics and Biases*, a collection of essays and research papers edited by Israeli social scientists Daniel Kahneman, Paul Slovic, and Amos Tversky, and published by Cambridge University Press (2002).

of reference points, information assumed to be accurate and relevant, external influences, and the little mental shortcuts we all employ in our daily choices.

Those who analyze financial decision making from the heuristic point of view employ terms such as *anchoring* to describe how people tend to form judgments based on false data and fallacious assumptions. For instance, during the 1990s tech frenzy, it was popular among investors to select Internet stocks based solely on price relative to the prices of others. Since high-tech issues were so hot, generally (providing the *anchor* or reference point for comparison), the assumption was that the best tech stock was the one currently selling at the lowest price, without regard to its fundamental value. Surely, it too would rise, and since it was starting from such a low point, it had the greatest prospects. Of course, the fallacy was revealed when tech stocks crashed across the board.

Another fallacy by which investors tend to find themselves misled is the idea that a good company necessarily equates with a good investment. This very conventional (herd-like) way of thinking reflects the common assumption that superior past performance will persist into the future. Investors flock to the shares of companies with strong track records, and conversely, avoid the stocks of underperformers. And why not? It would appear entirely logical to do so. But ironic though it may seem, studies demonstrate that stocks of unpopular companies with poor earnings records tend to outperform stocks of good companies with better records.

There are two reasons for this. The first phenomenon is *reversion to the mean*. This is the tendency of earnings growth rates to revert to a central, or *mean* number. It happens with the stocks of both good and bad companies. Second — and this is *very* significant — investors tend to be overly confident in their view of the future. Thus, they pay too high a price for superior historic earnings growth, assuming it will continue indefinitely, and too low a price for substandard earnings growth, ignoring the fact that this too can change.

Why should growth rates in earnings move from both extremes toward some central value? Because capital is mobile. Industries experiencing rapid earnings growth draw competition, bidding down returns on invested capital and slowing that growth. Whereas, industries experiencing stagnant earnings growth and low returns generally see capacity and competitors depart, leading to higher returns and resumed earnings growth for the companies remaining in the field (the speed with which this occurs is directly influenced by the barriers to entry, Buffett's "moat"). It is much easier for capital to move in and out of certain industries than others.

Because of the tendency for investors to overestimate their forecasting ability and underestimate the speed with which earnings growth reverts to the mean, companies with bright prospects (currently) get their shares bid up to premium prices. Whereas, those with temporarily clouded prospects are knocked down to depressed prices, even if they are perfectly solid in all other respects. But as share prices recover — owing to fundamentally good business characteristics — those undervalued stocks offer the prospects for superior return, while stocks of popular companies disappoint as unrealistic expectations are driven out of the price.[10]

The *good-company-equals-good-investment* assumption is one of those mental shortcuts that interest students of Behavioral Finance. It's another expression of human nature (related to herd psychology) that allow otherwise sensible people to arrive at false conclusions in a fairly predictable manner. And the long, sad history of bubbles and frenzies illustrates how strong it is — even among investment professionals.

Strangely, experienced financial specialists, whom you'd think would have the knowledge, experience and discipline to resist irrational impulses, can be as susceptible to the promptings of the mob as

---

10 This is the "art" behind Value Investing — buying unpopular stocks of companies with temporarily clouded prospects at a discount to their intrinsic value and riding the reversion wave, while avoiding popular stocks with seemingly rosy prospects.

It is possible to pay too much for anything, especially rosy prospects. Value Investing is difficult precisely because it requires investors to do what is counter-intuitive, unpopular and out of favor. Unpopular and temporarily depressed stocks will never make for good cocktail party bragging (they lack excitement), but they generally make better investments.

the casual market dabbler — in some cases, even more so. In fact, I've often thought they're the real lemmings of the investment world. Despite good educations received at Wharton, Harvard or other sophisticated business schools, as soon as they enter the profession, all too many of them fall readily into a uniform and self-reinforcing Wall Street mode of thinking. Institutional investors make much of their oft-stated intention to outpace the crowd, yet consistently, they seem to prefer behaving just like their colleagues — and it shows in the investment results they achieve.

They tend to make predictable buys of comfortable institutional stocks — those with the largest capitalizations, those followed by most other analysts, those that are most liquid — and to buy and sell in virtually identical, large quantities, following lockstep patterns of constant diversification in the clichéd (and mistaken) belief that diversity, in itself, guarantees good performance.

Rare indeed is the institutional investor who would step off the well-worn path to try a less conventional approach, for instance buying fewer issues in more concentrated positions of really fine companies (which is a favorite strategy of Warren Buffett and other truly great investment managers). It's the difference between buying a wide variety of cheap jug wines and buying select lots of good, though perhaps little-known, vintages which you feel are under-priced at the moment.

Most market pros have very little incentive to make such a contrarian call. The risk of professional damage looms too great if they should lose with an unconventional style or with a stock selection that is not ratified by popularity among their peers. They recoil at the possibility of being ridiculed, of looking like idiots. Because their aim is a long career in the highly conventionalized world of investments, failing conventionally (lemming-like) is preferable even to succeeding in an unconventional manner. It's an illustration of herd psychology, par excellence.

The Faith Dimension

The insights gained from neuroeconomic analysis point to what would be a very interesting line of inquiry. Monitoring and imaging have been used to track bodily responses and neural activity associated with religious practices like prayer and meditation, as well as to chart the physiological effects of ecstatic spiritual experiences and even of faith itself.[11] I'm not aware that anyone has ever attempted to compare these religion-related studies with research involving investor behavior, but I think it would be fascinating to see what similarities and differences might be observed.

This is not a frivolous speculation, because in a very real way, investing is a matter of faith. The idea that owning stock is a valid means of increasing wealth requires that you believe things can get better over time. And that is a fundamentally *religious* idea.

Someone with a spiritual turn of mind would express this assumption as confidence that God is in control and that He desires our betterment. If you don't have such an expressly religious outlook, think of it as believing in the idea of progress — believing that progress is *possible* — a kind of faith in itself, and similar enough to make my point.

Another way of looking at it is: *accepting that the system works* — which is to say, being able to believe that the market will eventually correctly price individual stocks, bringing them to levels that accurately reflect the values of the companies they represent. This is a matter of having faith in the collective wisdom of the millions of investors participating in the market, all of whom bring their own capabilities, perspectives and sources of information into the collective process.

Once you accept the validity of investing, you have to believe in the prospects of a particular company. I would hope that your confidence is based on solid data, but it still comes down to faith. Of course, you also have to believe in your data, and this in itself can pose a faith challenge that is formidable even for disciplined professionals

---

11 This research provides much of the information underlying a recently published book by University of Pennsylvania neuroscientist Andrew Newberg, MD, and therapist Mark Robert Waldman, *How God Changes Your Brain* (Ballantine Books, 2009).

who do research for a living. My associates frequently express their insecurities about the thoroughness of their company analyses.

I'll ask, "How much information do you feel you've collected on which to base your recommendation?"

"Oh, maybe 80 percent of what I want," is a typical answer.

"Eighty percent is good," I'll tell them. "Go ahead and make a decision."

"But I really wish I had more details," they'll reply. "Maybe I should keep digging."

"What you want is *certainty*," I'll say, "and certainty is impossible. Trust the work you've done, trust your instincts, and make your best judgment. Because the value of that last 20 percent [what economists call the *marginal utility*] won't really add much to the overall picture." (It may even allow an investor to develop an overly confident view of the future.) In other words, once you've learned how to make assessments about the evaluation of companies, and gained a reasonable amount of experience at it, have faith in your *ability* to do so.

Other religious ideas factor into investing as well, foremost among them the concept of eventual reward. Christians have never achieved unanimity in our understanding of how the *justice* of God balances off against His *mercy*. Ever since the Reformation, Protestants and Catholics have argued over what is the exact and proper relationship between acceptance of God's Grace and the need for human works in the attainment of Heaven (at various times they have argued that topic quite violently). Yet all believers seem to feel we're called upon to do *something*, and that God, in whatever measure of justice and mercy, will reward us, as long as our *works* reflect our *faith*.

In the realm of investing, the most basic thing we're called upon to do is exercise self-control. We have to accept the idea of *deferred gratification*, denying ourselves the tangible pleasures of spending in the here-and-now, and instead putting our money into these rather abstract instruments called stocks and bonds, which we hope will bring us a greater reward later. We have to believe it's worth the wait (which is a sort of earthbound equivalent to believing in Grace). And then we must choose good stocks and bonds, remain attentive to how our investments are performing, and make whatever adjustments are required as circumstances evolve (which is to say, we must exercise *diligence*, the investor's version of *works* in my theological analogy).

All this is a matter of *counting the cost*, which is the underlying theme in so many of Jesus' parables. If you're not able to commit yourself to these priorities, then investing makes no sense, and you might as well adopt the eat-drink-and-be-merry approach to economic life. Which is the approach a lot of people — being unable to discipline themselves in other ways — take to life in general. All I can advise in either case is that the costs of such profligacy are rather high in the end.

Making Sound Decisions

But this, too, is closely related to the unconscious aspect of our human nature — the religious/moral impulse being, in many ways, as sub-clinical as our responses to the prospects of gain or loss, or our susceptibility to influence by those around us. Which brings us back to Jason Zweig and his neurons. Once we accept the faith challenges posed by investing, how do we come to terms with those troublesome inner responses that seem to have a life all their own and can so readily make hash out of our economic hopes and expectations? The key is imposing structure on our decision making — Zweig calls it, *controlling the controllable* — so that we don't find ourselves struggling with important choices while being "whipsawed by the whims of the moment."[12]

Before you venture too deeply into the stock market, it's wise to invoke the ancient Greek aphorism attributed to Socrates (and a half dozen or more other ancient sages): "Know thyself." Get clear on what your financial expectations really are, and ask what level of risk you're willing to tolerate. If you're honest with yourself, you might discover you're not as intrepid as you thought you would be. But it's okay. This

---

12 Zweig offers a series of very useful suggestions that can limit the impact of neural responses on investment decisions, and aid you in making reasoned choices, beginning on page 75 (Chapter 4) of *Your Money & Your Brain*. My thoughts parallel many of his ideas.

is the sort of self-awareness I try to help my clients achieve early in our relationship. Such insights point to things you actually do want to know about yourself, and you're better off finding them out before you commit too much hard-earned cash and too many sleepless nights to the investing enterprise.

The next thing to do is to take a tip from the Boy Scouts and *be prepared.* Immerse yourself in the techniques which investment professionals use (though not in the herd psychology that too often overtakes them). At the very least, try to gain a general familiarity with the most common measures of corporate value noted in Chapter 5. Don't expect to develop expertise overnight. It takes years to become an experienced, competent stock analyst.

In an appendix to his book, Zweig provides a very savvy check list for investors just starting out (or for those wishing to correct bad stock-picking habits) in the form of the acronym, "THINK TWICE."[13] It's a series of wise tips worth quoting from:

Take the global view. Keep calm by using a spreadsheet that emphasizes your total net worth — not the changes in each holding. Before you buy a stock or mutual fund, check to see whether it overlaps what you already own....

Hope for the best, but expect the worst. Being braced for disaster — by diversifying [your holdings] and by learning market history — can help keep you from panicking. Every good investment performs badly some of the time. Intelligent investors stick around until the bad turns back to good.

Investigate, then invest. A stock is not just a price; it's a piece of a living corporate organism. Study the company's financial statements. Read a mutual fund's prospectus before you buy....

Never say always. No matter how sure you are that an investment is a winner, don't put more than 10 percent of your portfolio in it....

13 *Your Money & Your Brain*, pages 266-267. Reproduced with permission of the author.

Know what you don't know. Don't believe you are already an expert. Compare stock fund returns against the overall market and across different time periods. Ask what might make this investment go down; find out if the people pushing it have their own money in it.

The past is not prologue. On Wall Street, what goes up must come down, and what goes way up usually comes down with a sickening crunch. Never buy a stock or mutual fund just because it has been going up....

Weigh what they say. The easiest way to silence a market forecaster is to ask for the complete track record of all his predictions.... Before trying any strategy, gather objective evidence on the performance of others who have used it in the past.

If it sounds too good to be true, it probably is.... Anyone who offers high return at low risk in a short time is probably a fraud. Anyone who listens is definitely a fool.

Costs are killers. Trading costs can eat up 1 percent of your money per year, while taxes and mutual fund fees can take another 1 or 2 percent.... [C]omparison-shop and trade at a snail's pace.

Eggs go splat. So never put all your eggs in one basket. Spread your bets across U.S. and foreign stocks, bonds, and cash. No matter how much you like your job, don't put all your 401(k) into your own company's stock....

These are excellent guidelines to refer to when you feel the tug or clash of your neural responses. Keeping them before you (perhaps literally, taped to the edge of your computer monitor) can remind you to slow down, take a deep breath, and *think* before jumping into or out of some investment, putting money at imprudent risk, or foregoing a legitimate earning opportunity under the influence of raw emotion.

Hard as it may be to put into practice, Zweig's insight is correct: investors must learn to discriminate between the *reflexive* and the *reflective*. Doing so involves self-awareness and discernment (which is another religious idea, incidentally). Train yourself, and then practice,

practice, practice. Harvard economist Richard Zeckhauser makes an excellent suggestion along those lines: "Find cheap situations in which you can test your biases. Keep track in a hypothetical world of cheap experiments."[13] Another good bit of advice.

And don't forget, God has programmed our brains to help us survive and flourish. It's up to us to figure out how to use them most effectively.

---

13 *Your Money & Your Brain*, page 77.

chapter 5

Values & Value

In his Christmas address for 1952, Pope Pius XII shared an observation that has great relevance for investing (as, indeed, for other aspects of life). His late Holiness said, "It is above all a clear principle of wisdom that all progress is truly such if it knows how to add new conquests to old, to join new benefits to those acquired in the past — in a word, if it knows how to make capital out of experience."

Experience. Logical progression. Continuity. Building upon judgments and actions whose rightness has been borne out by events. This is the essence of maturity, and it is the perspective which investors bring — or *should* bring — to their task. It does not preclude the taking of risk which is so central to investment decisions. Rather, it helps in calibrating the prudence of the risks at hand. It forces you to focus on evaluating all the factors involved, and allows you to measure current options in light of the known results of previous choices. It is the antithesis of *gambling*, which is about trying to predict outcomes that are dependent on probability and random chance.

I was a child when Pius gave his wise advice, and I can't say his words made any impression on my second-grader's mind at the time. However, I have certainly built my adult career in accordance with his insights. I do not *gamble* on the stock market or pursue "tips" about "hot" stocks. I do not attempt to "time the market" from day to day. Rather, I seek investment opportunities whose promise can be substantiated by hard data. And while, as the advertising disclaimer always says, "Past performance does not guarantee future results," the success of my methodical and undramatic (some might even say *stodgy*) approach has been demonstrated over time. It reflects the moral wisdom which Pius XII was advocating, it has proven effective in my private investment-counseling practice, and it is particularly well suited to the management of mutual funds.

The Origins of Funds

I became interested in mutual funds early in my career, not least because of their interesting history. The prominence of mutual funds as popular investment vehicles is a fairly recent phenomenon, but the idea of pooling investors has a pedigree going back centuries.[1] The earliest-known instance of recruiting individuals into something resembling a mutual fund occurred in the Netherlands in 1774, when a merchant named Adriaan van Ketwich organized a trust that would invest in bonds from various countries, including Austria, Denmark, the German states, Spain, Sweden and Russia, as well as from colonial plantations in Central and South America.

The Dutch being given to moral aphorisms, van Ketwich adapted the national maxim, *Eendragt Maakt Magt* ("Unity Creates Strength") as the name of the fund, though no Dutch government bonds were included among its holdings. Van Ketwich also set an interesting ethical standard for fund operation by removing himself from day-to-day investment decisions, even while he functioned as the fund's manager. His intention was to avoid the appearance of any conflict of interest.

The success of the venture inspired other Dutch investment projects with similarly edifying names, such as *Voordeelig en Voorsigtig* ("Profitable and Prudent"), founded in 1776 by a group of Utrecht bankers, and van Ketwich's own 1779 follow-up, *Concordia Res Parvae*

---

1   K. Geert Rouwenhorst of the Yale School of Management's International Center for Finance, provides an excellent capsule history of how mutual funds came onto the financial scene in his paper, "The Origins of Mutual Funds" (2003), available online from the Social Science Research Network (http://papers.ssrn.com/sol3/papers.cfm?abstract_id =636146).

Crescunt ("Small Matters Grow by Consent"). The Netherlands' King William I was sufficiently intrigued by the potential of pooled investments to sponsor a fund in 1822. The Swiss took up the idea in the mid-1800s, followed by investors in England and other nations, including the thrifty Scots, who organized investor consortia in the 1880s. Such groups provided a goodly portion of the capital that fueled 19th-Century industrialization. And some of the earliest efforts proved quite durable, van Ketwich's *Voordeelig en Voorsigtig* trust remaining in operation for 114 years.

The fund concept first touched financial life in America when Dutch investors organized to acquire (at a significant discount and a substantial profit) the debt run up by the U.S. government during the Revolutionary War. But the first homegrown American investor pools were the Boston Personal Property Trust, formed in 1893, and the Alexander Fund, organized in Philadelphia in 1907. The Massachusetts Investors' Trust, established in Boston in 1924, was a true mutual fund in the modern sense, with participants holding a range of equities. It was the first of a group of mutual funds that allowed hordes of small investors to participate in the bull market of the 1920s.

The new mutual fund industry took its lumps like the rest of Wall Street in the 1929 crash. But under the close federal scrutiny that came with the advent of the SEC and a host of government regulations and investor protections, those funds that survived were gradually seen as the way for small investors to participate in the market and gain returns that generally kept well ahead of inflation. Over the years, different types of funds have appeared — including bond funds, money-market funds, index funds, hybrids and others — in response to the demand for asset diversity and to meet a wide array of investor objectives. According to the Investment Company Institute, by the end of 2007, there were more than 69,000 mutual funds worldwide.[2] And despite the recent market shocks, mutual funds in the U.S. still account for some $10 trillion in assets.

---

2 From ICI Factbook 2009 (available online at: http://www.ici.org/factbook/pdf/05_fb_table45.pdf).

Value Investing

The flagship in my Catholic fund group is the Ave Maria Catholic Values Fund, a name which can be read in two ways. First, because it is based on moral principles advocated by the Catholic Church, it clearly reflects recognizable *Catholic values*. At the same time, it incorporates the well established concept of *Value Investing*.[3]

This duality was not inadvertent. I practiced *Value Investing* long before I started the Ave Maria Funds. In fact, I would describe myself as a disciple of the world's greatest exponent of Value Investing, Warren E. Buffett.

Those who are familiar with Buffett may see this as something of a contradiction in one who advocates integrating Catholic values and investing. In his private life, Buffett champions values that are in extreme opposition to the Church's stance on a broad range of subjects. Buffett is strongly pro-choice on the issue of abortion, for instance. He adheres to an overall liberal social philosophy that, in many respects, is at wide variance from Church teaching. And I am not aware that religion figures to any degree at all in his selection of stocks.

My attraction to Buffett's investment techniques has elicited quizzical looks on more than one occasion, but I think the explanation I give makes perfect sense — to wit: *"Wayne Gretzky is probably the greatest hockey player in the last 30 years. But what if I found out he was pro-choice on abortion.* (In fact, I don't actually know where Gretzky stands on the question.) *Would I no longer say he was a great hockey player?* Life is complicated, and conflicting realities can exist side by side. Regardless of my feelings about someone's social views, I could never deny his accomplishments in the area of his professional expertise."

And so with Warren Buffett I cannot help but admire the manifest business acumen and investing skills that have built Berkshire Hathaway, Inc. his Omaha, Nebraska-based insurance and holding

---

3   It should be noted that the Ave Maria Mutual Funds are *Catholic* (that is, *universal*, the literal meaning of the word "catholic") in two other senses as well: (1) they survey a universe of investment options; and (2) they are available to all investors, not just members of the Roman Catholic Church.

company, into a premier U.S. financial institution. In Fall 2009, even after the market slide, its market capitalization was over $150 billion (Buffett owns 35 percent of the company), so the magnitude of Buffett's success is obvious. Value Investing is at the heart of this accomplishment, and I have tried to make his approach my own. As I explained the concept in my earlier book:

> "Value Investing consists of carefully analyzing all of the things of worth in a company, adding them up, subtracting the liabilities, and comparing the result to the price-per-share at which the company is trading in the marketplace. If the company's intrinsic business value is significantly greater than the market price of its shares, then that company is a logical investment candidate."[4]

The Value Investing method has served Buffett exceedingly well. His investment performance — 20 percent a year over 40 years — has been so spectacular that insurance regulators have permitted Berkshire Hathaway to maintain extraordinarily high levels of equities in its reserve portfolio. The result has been substantially greater reserves than any other insurance firm in the country.[5]

This dazzling performance has been reflected in the heights to which Berkshire stock has appreciated over the years. After hitting $147,000 per share in 2008, by December, 2009 Berkshire was selling at $100,000 per share. I have benefited directly from Buffett's success, having bought ten shares of Berkshire stock in 1981 at $600 per share. Over a period of two decades I sold off nine of those shares, mostly to pay for college tuition for my five kids. There's one share left, and I

---

4   *Shareholder Rebellion*, Page 15.

5   High investment returns have affected Berkshire Hathaway in another positive way. The company's debt is rated AA, having been downgraded from AAA in 2009, leaving only five companies in the nation rated AAA: Pfizer, Exxon, Automatic Data Processing, Johnson & Johnson and Microsoft. It should be noted that Berkshire's long-term success has been aided by the tax advantages that apply to insurance companies, of which Buffett has made several acquisitions. One of Berkshire Hathaway's insurance subsidiaries is GEICO.

plan to hold onto it indefinitely. It's price may be down right now, but I'm confident it will rise again.

Over the years, Buffett has acquired large holdings in such high-profile companies as Coca Cola, Walmart, American Express, U.S. Bank, Wells Fargo, and most recently, Burlington Northern Santa Fe — all good companies, with good products, well financed, and owing to his astute tracking of the market and adherence to Value Investing principles, bought at opportune times when prices were well below intrinsic value. Moreover, Buffett rarely sells a stock, preferring instead to add periodically to his accumulated holdings.

Value Investors like Buffett are not disturbed by fluctuations in the market. You can be sure that all the companies whose shares Buffett has acquired have experienced swings in price during the time he's held them, in some cases quite severe. He sees that as an opportunity, noting that, "volatility is your friend — it allows you to buy low." And overall, Buffett's purchases have trended upward, reflecting the appreciation in the value of the business underlying his shares.

A great generator of citable observations, Buffett often says he wouldn't care if share prices were totally unavailable for ten years, and the stock market closed down for that time. He's confident that the *value* of his stocks would rise, since they represent ownership of outstanding growing companies.[6] Apropos his Coca-Cola holdings, he's said that if he went to live on some other planet for 10 years, he'd find, when he returned to Earth, that Coke sales had continued to increase.

And his confidence is justified. Buffett does his homework. He's prudent, basing judgments on knowledge previously gained. He exer-

---

6   Buffett's investment understanding — indeed, Value Investing in general — is thoroughly grounded in the principle of *ownership*. Buffett never thinks of stocks as mere "pieces of paper" or of buying stock as "playing the market." He's a serious investor who understands and appreciates what he owns.

Warren Buffett isn't the only investor pursuing the Value approach. Other value investors I have admired and tried to emulate include: Mike Price of Mutual Shares; Chuck Royce of the Royce Family of Mutual Funds; Marty Whitman of Third Avenue Value Fund; Bob Rodriguez of First Pacific Advisors; John Keeley of Keeley Value Fund; and Scott Satterwhite and George Sertl of the Artisan Partners. Each of these highly astute investors has had an excellent long-term track record.

cises great patience in awaiting his opportunities or the "perfect pitch", as he calls it. One might even say that, perhaps without knowing he's doing so, Warren Buffett follows Pope Pius' advice, "making capital out of experience."

Evaluating Companies

How is value investing practiced? That is to say, how do you determine whether a particular company represents a good investment opportunity?

In order to answer that, we must first address a very common misuse of terms. Many people — including many investment professionals —speak of the current "value" of a stock, and in doing so, confuse the words *value* and *price*, using the two interchangeably. That's a mistake that can lead to all kinds of confusion (even to losing money in the market). Buffett distinguishes between the two words in this way: "'Price,'" he explains, "is what you *give*, while 'value' is what you *get*." To put it another way, you can purchase a stock at a 50-percent discount from its value, which means its *price* is half its *value* — a good buy, because the price still has the potential to rise. Sometimes the price of a stock exceeds its value, which means the price has already risen beyond any reasonable estimate of the company's value. It's overpriced, and so its price has to fall to reach its value.

With this distinction made, there are several statistical methods of assessing the intrinsic value of a business. Three traditional measures are...

1. Liquidation Value (LV) — the expected proceeds if a company were to be dissolved and its assets sold and liabilities paid off (a related measure is 'breakup value,' the combined LV of all the various components if they were sold off piecemeal).

2. Net Present Value (NPV) — the value of all future cash flows which the business is expected to generate, discounted back to the present at an appropriate discount rate (the "discount," being an adjustment for the purchasing power of the currency over that

period, or what is commonly referred to as the "time value" of money).

3. Private Market Value (PMV) — a comparison with sale prices when other firms within the same commercial sector change ownership. Much like real estate assessors look for comparable transactions to arrive at an estimate of value, this is a valuation based upon price comparisons with transactions in which entire businesses, in similar industries, change hands.[7]

While all three of these measures are objective, they each involve comparisons, projections and assumptions which, by their nature, are imprecise, indefinite, subject to change, open to interpretation, and somewhat less than fully tangible (for instance, when trying to determine PMV, it can be hard to find other companies similar enough to make true apples-to-apples comparisons). It is an irony of business that for these standards of valuation to gain in substance and credibility, they must be viewed in light of something that is even less tangible but absolutely essential in determining the worth of a company: goodwill.

Goodwill is image, reputation, trust, the relationship between a company and its customers. It is how a business is perceived, thought about, referred to, depended upon. Goodwill includes public awareness of the company's products or services, recognition of its brand names and trademarks. It is a firm's standing, relative to the competition. It is, in essence, all the things related to human consciousness, appeal and motivation that are intangible in the extreme, but nonetheless so important that the success of a company — indeed its very survival — depends on them. Goodwill is a monetary reality. It's difficult to calculate, but there are many instances where the value of goodwill is the most critical (even the largest) number in the value assessment. It's why you buy Coke instead of just "Cola."[8]

---

7   For instance, the price at which companies in the publishing field sell has historically been 10 times annual cash flow, but a lot lower today.

8   In accounting, the term "goodwill" has a very specific meaning. It refers to the amount paid in excess of the book value of a company when a firm is acquired. That's not what I mean here by "goodwill." I'm talking about those intangibles related to the perception of a company by the public.

No statistical measure can fully determine a company's potential as an investment without considering goodwill — which generally makes Liquidation Value a very incomplete measure of a company's worth. LV is concerned only with the property, hardware, inventory and cash that remain after a business has ceased operations. It is accounting taken to the far edge of minimalism, a tally of inanimate assets divorced from human action. In a sense, it's a projection of failure, showing you only what you'll have if the business goes belly-up — useful in providing a worst-case perspective, but of limited helpfulness in measuring the potential of a growing company in which long-term investors might wish to put their money.

Net Present Value, on the other hand, does take goodwill into account, because it's based on cash flow, which can only be generated by the interplay of a company and its market (in which goodwill is an essential component). The same with Private Market Value, since PMV measures the worth of an active company against the prices paid for other firms doing business in the same general field of endeavor.

None of these measures is flawless in its ability to indicate which stocks will rise in price over time. Each can be criticized in various ways. For instance, determining a company's NPV depends on the ability to reliably predict future cash flows — which experience shows often turns out to be an exercise in tea-leaf reading, since the future is infinitely variable. Business conditions change, as do consumer tastes and patterns in customer behavior. Unanticipated problems arise. Important personnel come and go according to shifts in individual circumstances.

What's more, statistical calculations, divorced from other information about a company, can be profoundly misleading. They can put a false appearance of good investment potential on stocks that are really what Buffett, in his colorful way, calls cigar butts. These are stocks that seem attractively cheap, but unfortunately, wind up staying cheap for years, because, in reality, the companies behind them aren't well managed, profitable or growing — they lack *good business characteristics.* But if numbers, in themselves, don't tell the whole story, they do tell quite a lot. Each methodology has its strengths, and they're all arrows in a stock analyst's quiver. Taken together, these techniques allow skill-ful analysts to paint a useful picture. Recent years have seen the intro-duction of a fourth analytical methodology, more refined than Liquidation Value, Net Present Value or Private Market Value, based on the equation:

$$\frac{EV}{EBITDA}$$

This procedure divides a company's Enterprise Value (EV) — its *capitalization*, the total market value of its stock plus its outstanding long-term debt[9] by its gross cash flow, defined as its "EBITDA" (Earnings Before Interest, Taxes, Depreciation and Amortization), to arrive at a ratio. Typically, the lower the ratio of EV to EBITDA, the more attractive the stock price for purchase. Everything else being equal, a company whose Enterprise Value is five times EBITDA would be a better investment prospect than one where EV is 10 times EBITDA.

Other Considerations

Beyond the numbers, there are other factors to consider when eval-uating prospective investments. For instance, Warren Buffett looks for whether a company has some unique aspect that helps to protect its position in the marketplace from the assaults of competition — what he calls a moat (as in the moat around a castle). One factor that con-stitutes a moat is brand equity, the high level of consumer awareness and loyalty that can sustain product popularity over time. In a sense, a brand is the ultimate expression of goodwill. Implicit in a well estab-lished brand is a promise of what will be delivered to the person buy-ing that product — what brings the customer back time after time.

Brand equity would have been an especially compelling factor in Buffett's purchases of Coca-Cola stock (100 million shares that later

---

9   Enterprise Value includes both the aggregate market value of a company's stock (its equi-ty) and its long-term debt, because equity and debt together represent what the company is considered to be worth in the marketplace.

split two-for-one). Coke is a global icon with market visibility and consumer attachment maintained for more than a century. Every year, Coke is ranked as the world's most valuable brand. It has such a high level of recognition that its trademark elements, the famous cursive-script logo and contour bottle have been altered little since Coca-Cola was first introduced as a packaged consumer product.[10]

Another factor that can function as a moat is a firm's Unique Proprietary Position (UPP) in its market. A company like Walmart might be said to have a UPP. Walmart stores not only benefit from a well established brand identity, they are often the only big-box retailers in the communities where they're located (until recent years, mainly in small towns and suburban areas). They offer such a comprehensive array of products at such comparatively low prices that independent competitors find themselves under severe pressure, often to the point of closure. Walmart regularly faces community resistance — right up to mob-in-the-street protests — over that power to revolutionize local economies. So much so that it's become almost fashionable to dislike Walmart, and nearly everyone does — that is, except for the roughly 100 million Walmart shoppers (in the U.S. alone).

Simple market dominance can have a moat-like effect, at least for awhile, though the past quarter-century-or-so has demonstrated just how fleeting dominance can be. We've witnessed a series of *whiz-bang* technology firms, each with some impressive new product, system or process, bursting onto the scene, dominating its market for a time, then being swept aside by some other, even more dazzling digital

---

10 You'll likely make good money buying the stocks of companies with super-strong brands — that is, *if* you don't pay too much. Price is the key. And the challenge in acquiring the shares of such companies is that, generally speaking, price gets down to the "bargain" level only when something goes terribly wrong.

The greatest buying opportunity in the history of Coca-Cola was 1985 when the infamous "New Coke" was introduced. The reformulation of Coke's traditional ingredient mix (premiered with much fanfare to combat market inroads by other soft drinks, primarily rival Pepsi) so infuriated loyal customers as to cause protests and black-market importation of Coke bottled outside the U.S., where the new version hadn't yet been launched. Coke shares took an uncharacteristic tumble, and anyone who bought at the depressed price was amply rewarded when the original formula was resurrected as "Coca-Cola Classic" and the stock rebounded.

gizmo (Does the name Atari sound vaguely familiar?). Likewise, even venerable firms that were top-of-mind when it came to meeting specialized needs have seen dominance vanish. Remember Pan-Am or TWA, both in their time virtually synonymous with overseas travel? If not, then ask the U.S. carmakers how well they're dominating the automotive world these days.

When I was a boy, General Motors had 55 percent of the auto market in the U.S. and was actually threatened with anti-trust action by the government because of its near-monopolistic dominance. It was the very model of a profitable, multi-national corporation, with AAA-rated bonds in such demand that investors would pay nearly as much for them as for gilt-edged U.S. Treasury securities.[11] Today, with barely 20 percent of the U.S. market and billions in annual losses, GM has gone bankrupt and been partially nationalized through the infamous and ill-advised government bailout (really a bailout of the UAW by the strongly pro-union Obama Administration).[12]

Well, if the crumbling state of U.S. automakers demonstrates that nothing lasts forever, there is at least one factor that can offer some protection of market position — at least for awhile, anyway. That is a growing stream of sales and earnings. The key is *trend*. In his stock analyses, Buffett doesn't just look for good current performance, he wants to see the line going up over an extended period of time. That kind of continuing growth, projected against the other measures used in the Value Investing method can suggest the presence of a moat, marking a good investment prospect.

Related to sales and earnings, of course, is profitability. Buffett is interested in companies with low debt (an *unleveraged* balance sheet).

---

11 In the 1950s and '60s, GM bonds traded at yields only slightly above those of U.S. Treasury bonds, and this despite the fact that the federal government, with the power to print money, could guarantee its securities would always pay off — an advantage GM didn't have.

12 I have long believed that GM's equity was, quite literally, *given away* to retirees and the United Auto Workers Union through labor contracts that were overly generous, to say the least. If ever there was a situation that justified — that, in fact, *demanded* — stockholder action, clearly it is this willful destruction of America's single greatest industrial enterprise.

High return on equity means that the company doesn't have to take on debt or issue more stock to raise the capital it needs to refurbish plant and equipment, pay dividends, or make acquisitions. Being debt-free also allows a company to buy back its own shares on the open market.[13]

Truly profitable companies (think Microsoft or Apple) finance their own operations and growth with *free cash flow*[14] (defined as profit plus depreciation expenses that are in excess of maintenance and capital expenditures). This shows that a company can pay its own way — a sign that it likely has good business characteristics and, especially, good management. I have always stressed the importance of owning shares of financially strong companies, a view which has been vindicated by the 2008-09 recession.

Such financial powerhouses — usually debt-free, with highly liquid balance sheets — have control of their own destinies in ways that leveraged companies do not. The overleveraging of Corporate America has been well documented. During the economic prosperity of the 90s, many companies leveraged their financial structures with loads of debt. More recently, banks adopted the practice in the form of *subprime* lending.

When business is good, leverage can be an effective strategy. Taking on debt allows a company to exploit earning opportunities that yield a greater return than would have been possible without the debt. The problem comes when things slow down. All that borrowing means interest expense that takes a huge bite out of profits already adversely affected by contracting revenues. In late 2009, as the U.S. economy emerged from the worst recession since the 1930s, investors were once more awakening to the dangers of excessive corporate debt and, conversely, to the benefits of being debt-free.

Debt-free companies have a much greater ability to weather economic storms, even continuing to grow stronger during recessions.

---

13 A company should buy back its stock only when share price is depressed. I am always agitated when boards recklessly decide to repurchase their own shares at inflated prices.

14 Free cash flow is an important factor relative to stock price. A Value Investor would want to buy at a price that is low in relation to the free cash flow of the company.

They can continue to make investments in capital improvements, and research and development for new products. They can expand through acquisition of properties, products or entire businesses, often buying from distressed sellers at bargain prices. If their own stock is depressed because of short-term market factors, they can use cash reserves to repurchase their own shares on the cheap. Because of their staying power, strong companies can opportunistically steal customers from the weak, putting nails in the coffins of their faltering competitors. Financially powerful companies use recessions to build for the future and enhance, if not guarantee, earnings growth when prosperity returns, advantageously using liquid resources during periods of general economic weakness to create permanent shareholder value.

In contrast, companies that are overburdened by debt — the financial weaklings — have trouble managing cash flow. They are forced to cut back on capital expenditures and R&D, hurting their competitive positions with long-term detrimental consequences. They often find themselves forced by their bankers to make drastic cuts in spending, personnel and product planning, or else they resort to the stopgap measure of raising equity capital at the worst possible time, diluting shareholders' interests.

While low debt is never an absolute guarantee that a company's stock is a good investment, it is almost always a characteristic of a high-quality company. Usually, it's a residual of a really good business with proprietary products and good profit margins, operating in a growth market and blessed with good management. And when the shares of such fine companies are out of favor and depressed, they can be superb investments.

Another factor that rates high in Buffett's assessment of potential investments is demonstrated integrity among corporate managers — having to do with the ethical standards by which a company is run, rather than with any other moral or religious considerations (I'm not referring here to the concept of Morally Responsible Investing). Are the company's managers forthright and open in their dealings with shareholders? Buffett values candor. Does executive compensation accurately reflect company performance? Managers getting rich at the expense of the shareholders — rather than as a justified consequence of demonstrated success — is a red flag. Consistent with his views on compensation, Buffett never issues stock options to Berkshire Hathaway executives. Rather, he's known for paying his people well, giving them ample bonuses, and encouraging them to buy Berkshire stock on the open market with their own after-tax dollars, just as any other investor would.

The most important factor in shopping for stock, of course, is price, and that's always a moving target.[15] Buffett is the archetype of the *contrarian* investor. He buys world-class companies that are well managed and have strong finances, but that are temporarily out of favor. He took a big position in Wells Fargo, the banking and financial services company, back in the '90s, when banks faced severe problems and S&Ls were blowing up everywhere. At the height of 2008's wildest market fluctuations, when investors were running in circles from pure panic, Buffett wrote an op-ed piece for The *New York Times* in which he offered a bit of strikingly contrarian advice: "Buy American! I am."

> "A simple rule dictates my buying: Be fearful when others are greedy, and be greedy when others are fearful. And most certainly, fear is now widespread, gripping even seasoned investors. To be sure, investors are right to be wary of highly leveraged entities or businesses in weak competitive positions. But fears regarding the long-term prosperity of the nation's many sound companies make no sense. These businesses will indeed suffer earnings hiccups, as they always have. But most major companies will be setting new profit records 5, 10 and 20 years from now."[16]

Naturally, timing is critical to the success of Buffett's contrarian practices. A good buy isn't a good buy forever, only when conditions make it so. And conditions never stay the same. Life goes on. But

---

15 It's important to note that price is relative. A stock may be selling at a price you would consider high in absolute terms, and yet still be a good buy. You have to compare price with other factors, as in the famous "price/earnings ratio."

16 *The New York Times*, October 16, 2008.

Buffett would insist that trying to "time" the market is a loser's game. There are speculators who sit in front of computer screens all daylong, jumping in and out of closely followed stocks trying to make a quick turn on the movement of a point or two. But such people are gamblers, not true investors.

Roots of the Approach

As *I* follow the principles of Warren Buffett, so *he* was influenced by Benjamin Graham, his mentor at Columbia University's Business School in the 1940s. Graham co-wrote, with Columbia colleague, David L. Dodd, the classic investment text, *Security Analysis*,[17] considered the seminal work of the Value Investing philosophy. Appearing in 1934, the book drew on lessons learned in the 1929 stock market crash and the then-unfolding Great Depression. As noted in an article taken from the online reference source, "Wikipedia":

> "Graham and Dodd chided Wall Street for its myopic focus on a company's reported earnings per share, and were particularly harsh on the favored 'earnings trends.' They encouraged investors to take an entirely different approach by gauging the rough value of the operating business that lay behind the security. Graham and Dodd enumerated multiple actual examples of the market's tendency to irrationally under-value certain out-of-favor securities. They saw this tendency as an opportunity for the savvy.[18]

---

17 *Security Analysis* was first published by Whittlesey House, a division of McGraw-Hill. It has been updated in four later editions, with the latest reprint issued in 2004. I'm pleased to own a leather-bound limited-edition copy with a foreword by Buffett. On one of my trips to Omaha, I was able to have him sign it for me.

18 From Wikipedia, as updated October 9, 2008, — http://en.wikipedia.org/wiki/Security_Analysis_(book). The Wikipedia entry links to an interesting 1976 interview in *Financial Analysts Journal*, where Graham says that in the years since *Security Analysis* appeared, he had somewhat shifted his analytical emphasis to focus on groups of stocks. His remarks are available online at: http://www.bylo.org/bgraham76.html.

Security Analysis built on a long tradition of attempting to apply empirically verified analytical techniques to investing judgment which had reached its zenith with publication of the "Dow Theory" in 1902. Created by Charles H. Dow, co-founder of *The Wall Street Journal,* the theory maintained that stock prices could be charted — and thus, buying and selling decisions made — by tracking three types of price activity. As explained by Dow's protégé, William Peter Hamilton, who further refined the theory...

> "Simultaneously in any broad stock market there are — acting, reacting and interacting — three definite movements. That on the surface is the daily fluctuation; the second is a briefer movement typified by the reaction in a bull market or the sharp recovery in a bear market which has been oversold; the third and main movement is that which decides the trend over a period of many months, or the main true movement of the market."[19]

Dow's theory had a "macro" perspective, based as it was on the Dow Jones Averages, the composite index of selected railroad and industrial stocks he had created. Graham and Dodd, on the other hand, focused on achieving a more definitive assessment of the particular strengths and weaknesses of individual corporations, whose prospects might contrast dramatically with general market performance.

> "At bottom, *Security Analysis* stands for the proposition that a well-disciplined investor can determine a rough value for a

---

19 William Peter Hamilton elaborated on the principles of the Dow Theory over two decades in a series of commentaries in *The Wall Street Journal.* Extracts of his writings (like the one cited above) were included in a booklet titled, *The Dow Theory,* written by Robert Rhea and published originally in 1932 by the investment firm, Rhea, Greiner & Co. (and reprinted continuously over the next 30 years).

While the effectiveness of Charles Dow's theory as a market predictor has been questioned and various other stock indexes have appeared on the scene, the Dow Jones Industrial Average remains the most common, general-purpose measure of market performance. Its daily closing figure is still the first answer given to the question, "How did the market do today?"

company from all of its financial statements, make purchases when the market inevitably under-prices some of them, earn a satisfactory return, and never be in real danger of permanent loss. Warren Buffett, the only student in Graham's investment seminar to earn an A+ ... made billions of dollars by methodically and rationally implementing the tenets of Graham and Dodd's book."[20]

So indeed he did. And throughout my own career, I have attempted to profit from Buffett's example and the insights he gained at the knee of Benjamin Graham — to "make capital out of experience," as it were. I like to think Pope Pius XII would be pleased.

Warren Buffett's one "religious" reference (at least, the only one of which I'm aware) expresses a great financial truth in a humorous way: "The market, like the Lord, helps those who help themselves. But, unlike the Lord, the market does not forgive those who know not what they do." In other words, investing successfully requires information. More to the point, it requires thorough and specific information. I related a very telling anecdote in my earlier book:

> "Going to Thanksgiving dinner at a friend's house one year, I mentioned I'd bring a couple of bottles of very nice Nouveau Beaujolais. My friend said, "Oh, if it's that nice, can you bring me a case? I'll set some aside." But the fact is Nouveau Beaujolais must be drunk in the year it was bottled — usually by mid-December of that year — or it turns to vinegar. I brought my friend some Cabernet Sauvignon instead. She knew enough about wine to know that some of it improves with age, but she didn't know enough to realize that Nouveau Beaujolais is an exception. People make the same kind of mistakes with investments every day."[21]

---

20 From Wikipedia, as updated October 9, 2008,—http://en.wikipedia.org/wiki/Security_Analysis_(book)

21 *Shareholder Rebellion*, page 17.

It's like the old saying, "A little knowledge is a dangerous thing," as all too many market dabblers have discovered to their chagrin.

Digging out the facts on which to base sensible investment decisions takes hard work. I have a staff of Chartered Financial Analysts (all of them with MBAs) pursuing information on prospective investments all day every day. They read annual reports, press releases, 10Ks and 10Qs (government-required disclosure forms), are all highly educated, highly trained, talented, motivated (well paid) and experienced. They analyze balance sheets and income statements, contact managements and visit selected corporate headquarters and branch offices. They attend conferences where company managers make investor presentations, and then they sit down with those executives for face-to-face interviews in breakout sessions. Then, all this primary research is supplemented by secondary research obtained from national brokerages and regional boutiques.

Some Guidelines

This is security analysis done at a high level of sophistication. But whether or not individuals avail themselves of such professional service, there are guidelines of which they should be aware. Inspired by Buffett and distilled over my 40 years in the field, these are the basics, a few simple precepts that can at least point you in a productive direction when you're making investment decisions.[22]

1. ERR ON THE SIDE OF CONSERVATISM. Don't let hope or optimism color your reading of the facts. If anything, understate your assessments. For instance, if you're attempting to estimate value by applying the traditional measures, LV, NPV and PMV, use the lowest of the three, or a low average with emphasis on NPV. As Benjamin Graham advised, leave a margin of safety — a

---

22 These points were discussed in my earlier book. I revisit them after a decade and a half of additional experience and the development of the Ave Maria funds — and also in light of how I've set forth my thoughts in this current work. So these are not word-for-word quotations from *Shareholder Rebellion*.

large margin (think of it as building a bridge strong enough to carry a 30,000-pound truck, but then only being willing to drive a 10,000-pound truck over it).

2. KNOW THE FIELD IN WHICH YOU WISH TO INVEST. Over the years, my firm has concentrated on businesses we know well. We've had a particular interest in financial services (banks, thrifts and insurance companies), healthcare, auto after-market companies, and manufacturers of certain proprietary products. Buffett calls it operating within your sphere of competency.

3. CHECK OUT YOUR OWN BACKYARD. Any number of investment opportunities can present themselves right in your own area, and proximity makes it easier to get to know the folks minding the store. Since we're headquartered in suburban Detroit, we frequently go out and "kick the tires" of companies we're following in Michigan or the adjoining states of Indiana and Ohio. To quote the famous sermon, sometimes there are "acres of diamonds" in your own backyard.[23]

4. BE A CONTRARIAN. You can't always know when is the "perfect" time to buy, but if you're minimally aware of trends, you can make reasonable projections. It's like the old saw about buying straw hats in January, when they're cheap, in anticipation of making a profit selling them when demand is up in July. We made a great *contrarian* investment for our clients some years ago, at a time when healthcare was looming as an issue on the political horizon. It was a Michigan company called MEDSTAT, which did outcomes analysis for healthcare organizations. We realized this service would be increasingly important, but at the time, MEDSTAT's principal asset, its database, didn't even appear on its balance sheet. We started buying shares, and were rewarded years later, when the stock soared as the result of a buyout by a Canadian

---

23 "Acres of Diamonds," by Rev. Russell H. Conwell (1843-1925), Baptist minister, lecturer, and founder of Philadelphia's Temple University.

company. The return for our clients was more than six times their average costs.

5. BE PATIENT. Value Investing is like farming. You cultivate, you sow, you water, you wait. It takes time before the crop comes in. Just so, the Value Investor needs farmer-like patience and persistence — which I can tell you from years of personal experience. We make investments just about every day, but we sell only occasionally. As in the MEDSTAT example, above, eventually you reap the harvest.

To sum up, investing is not gambling. It's work — *hard* work — and you will make mistakes doing it. But with seriousness, maturity, dedication, and a willingness to take risks, you can learn and you can "make capital out of experience."

chapter 6

Politics & Markets

This book attempts to make connections between religious faith and financial prudence. Unquestionably, politics impinges on both, and perhaps that's inevitable. America was born largely out of human strivings that are religious at the core, and those strivings continue. Over the centuries, masses of people have come to these shores driven by the dual hopes of worshiping in freedom and improving the material conditions of their lives. The interplay of Church, marketplace and government is at the heart of the American story, and it always will be. With that perspective — which is intrinsically moral — it might be worthwhile to look more closely at how the recent spasms of economic pain and political hubbub have come upon us.

It was something of a shock to read the headlines about a Spring 2009 *Rasmussen Reports* opinion poll in which a razor-thin majority of respondents (only 53 percent) declared their preference for capitalism over socialism. How could it be — 20 years after the fall of the Berlin Wall and the collectivist, police-state nightmare it had so long symbolized — that Americans weren't more convinced about the virtues of an economic system that thwarted the world-domination aims of the "Evil Empire?" Had the recession so shaken our confidence? Were we really so shallow and thoughtless as a people? Were memories that short?

Parsing the poll numbers more closely, it becomes apparent that age played a significant part in framing the 53-percent figure. Respondents under 30 favored capitalism only 37 percent to 33 percent, with 30 percent undecided. At the same time, 49 percent of those in the thirty-something age group went for capitalism, against 26 percent for socialism, a considerably wider spread. The 40-plus crowd was in favor of capitalism overwhelmingly; only 13 percent went for socialism.[1]

What this poll actually reveals is the extent to which the distinctions between capitalism and socialism — two inherently conflicting visions of personal and economic liberty — have been blurred by mass media and an educational system given over to the false notion of *moral equivalence*. It was frequently asserted, back during the days of the Cold War, that the United States and the Soviet Union were basically "two sides of the same coin." This view has persisted stubbornly in certain intellectual and creative circles, in spite of all evidence to the contrary.[2]

As a result, people too young to have seen the reports of Soviet oppression, and those whose understanding has been dulled by propaganda of the *Why-can't-we-all-just-get-along?* variety are least likely to

---

1   *Rasmussen Reports*, Thursday, April 9, 2009. Not surprisingly, investors as a group preferred capitalism by a margin of five to one, while 25 percent of non-investors had a warm spot for socialism.

2   If you'd like to refresh your memory about how the leftish intellectual establishment once portrayed the U.S. and U.S.S.R. as essentially the same (and taking such a stroll down "Memory Lane" would be a very worthwhile exercise), I recommend a book titled, *Scorpions in a Bottle*, published in 1989 by Hillsdale College Press. This slim volume offers presentations from a conference held the previous year in Washington, D.C. examining misperceptions about the struggle with totalitarian Communism. It features marvelous insights from William Bennett, Sidney Hook, Jeane Kirkpatrick, Irving Kristol, Melvin Lasky, Michael Novak, and other perceptive observers of the period.

     It's fascinating to see how certain "deep thinkers" continue to deny that there is anything uniquely virtuous in America's way of life. Since the Soviet Union took its much-deserved place in history's dustbin, the "moral equivalence" argument has been given a wider focus in an effort to pooh-pooh all suggestions that the United States offers greater personal freedom or economic opportunity than other societies. This in spite of the fact that downtrodden people from all over the world continue to "vote with their feet" by emigrating from their oppressed home countries to America.

recognize as unique and indispensable the system that has brought the United States its unparalleled freedom and prosperity. In fact, they have only the vaguest notion of what capitalism and socialism are — a truth made evident by an earlier poll that noted a full 70-plus-percent favorable rating for a "free-market economy" (as opposed to "capitalism"). How you phrase the question matters.

Make no mistake: socialism is not a "third way" of organizing economic life. It is, in fact, merely a lesser degree of government centralization than Soviet Communism. Economies are distinguished by who owns and controls property and resources — as Marx put it, the "means of production." Either *people* are the owners (individually or as corporate groups), or *governments* are the owners. Ownership by people allows for the exchange of assets, which makes goods and services available through payments of money or other units of value. Producers profit, and consumers obtain the things they need and desire. Ownership by government, or the imposition of stifling government regulation, subsidization, or production "priorities," disrupts free exchange, or even precludes it altogether.

This is a critical point. The capitalist system provides a variety of incentives for people to produce things which other people are willing to pay for. When government is the producer — or even when government interferes with transactions between producers and consumers — incentives are reduced or destroyed, production declines, and scarcity increases. This is not only an economic failure, it is a moral failure, because human needs are not met.

The Politics of Change

The obscuring of such basic truth was undoubtedly a factor in the broad support for the candidacy of Barack Obama. The first year of the Obama Administration has given substance to the fears expressed by conservatives that this onetime community activist would be the most socialist-inclined president of all time. Obama's moves toward nationalizing wide swaths of banking, finance, health, manufacturing and other sectors of the economy are far bolder than anything attempted even by Franklin Roosevelt in his Constitution-blind, Supreme Court-packing heyday.

The shape of this "change" which Obama promised is pretty much what could have been inferred from the facts that were known about the candidate. Obama really did very little to mask his association with the Bill Ayers/Acorn/George Soros radical vanguard. In some ways, he conducted the most transparent campaign in recent memory. He only distanced himself from Rev. Jeremiah Wright after his longtime pastor's inflammatory preaching began to diminish the candidate's "post-racial" luster.

There's nothing new about Americans electing an idealized figure who turns out to be something other than the paragon of leadership anticipated. For instance, Jimmy Carter proved quite a bit less than what was suggested by his background as an officer on nuclear submarines. But in the 2008 election, we watched a majority of voters — abetted by the mainstream media — choosing to be willfully ignorant of the forces that had shaped Obama's attitudes, even though the candidate's history was well known and the people whose influence was greatest upon him were all in plain view.

Those who are still mesmerized by the "audacity of hope" may cling to their denial, but the cracks in Obama's base of support have widened considerably. An April 2009 opinion poll conducted jointly by the Associated Press and GFK/Roper showed less than half (48 percent) of respondents expressing their feeling that the country was headed in the "right direction."[3] This research was conducted in the days immediately after the first wave of "Tea Parties" held around the country to protest the administration's tax priorities and bail-out programs. Obama's good friends in the media did their best to fudge this unflattering situation. CNN had an interesting take. Reporting on its own survey (conducted jointly with Opinion Research Corp.), CNN headlined: "Obama More Popular than His Policies, Poll Shows."[4]

---

3   Archived online at: http://www.ap-gfkpoll.com.

4   "Obama More Popular than His Policies, Poll Shows." CNNPolitics.com, for Monday, April 27, 2009 (archived online at: http://www.cnn.com/2009/POLITICS/04/27/poll.obama.policies/).

Yes, well — that was one way to look at it. The conservative *Washington Times* took a somewhat different view, citing a survey taken by the Gallup Organization showing that, at the fabled "First-100-Days" point, Barack Obama, with a 56-percent approval rate, was the second *least* popular new President in the 40 years these measures have been taken.[5] He was behind his much-reviled predecessor, George W. Bush, behind Richard Nixon, behind Jimmy Carter. Only Bill Clinton was less popular at the 100-day mark in his White House tenure — and that was because of the ill-fated assault on the Branch Davidian complex in Waco, Texas.

By late summer 2009, the economy's slow response to all the stimulus money, coupled with grassroots rebellion against Democrat proposals for healthcare reform, had sent Obama's numbers into steep decline, and polling showed that in nearly every state more voters identified themselves as "conservative" than those who claim the "liberal" designation — no doubt a severe disappointment to the president who had promised all that "change." By December 2009, a Gallup Poll showed Obama's overall approval rating had slipped to the low 40s, a record low for any president at that point in his presidency.

I reluctantly place myself in the position of Rush Limbaugh, inviting the kind of vile and unfounded criticism he received for his opposition to Obama.[6] In the manner of Rush, I hope the President's initiatives fail. That is to say, I hope they fail to retard the natural recovery that will happen in spite of his overblown plans, once we have passed through the painful but necessary economic contraction that has followed (and was an outgrowth of) the bursting of the Federal Reserve-induced housing bubble. To that extent: I applaud the protestors who so impolitely discomfited our poor senators and congresspersons at

5   "Barack's in the Basement," The Washington Times, Tuesday, April 28, 2009 (archived online at: http://washingtontimes.com/news/2009/apr/28/baracks-in-the-basement).

6   Contrary to the false picture which the Obama-friendly mainstream media tried to paint, Rush Limbaugh never said he hoped the President would fail. What he hoped was that Obama would fail to move the nation in the direction of socialism. Not that Rush suffered from the misinterpretation of his remarks — listenership of his daily radio program soared.

their summer-recess townhall meetings; I cheer GOP resistance, and hope it proves effective; and I pray for a reassertion of good sense among politicians of all stripes who understand the real source of our national abundance (God), the essence of our political/economic system (individual liberty), and the true need of current politics (honesty and accountability). If this amounts to a failure of Democrats and the most ideological aspects of their agenda, then I'll take it and bear any criticism that may come.

Anatomy of a Bubble

The meltdown of 2008-09 was not primarily brought on because of the vaunted Wall Street *excesses* of which we've heard so much. Important though they may have been, they were effects and symptoms of a much more fundamental cause, which was the depth to which politics had penetrated the financial markets. The driving force behind our recent debacle was a combination of power-lust, hypocrisy and money, an unholy trinity that appears again and again throughout political history.

A key component in the market washout was the collapse of housing prices, which obliterated billions of dollars in home equity and undermined the stability of the mortgage-backed securities that are the mainstay of the home-finance industry. This precipitated a very typical panic in which both individual and institutional investors rushed wildly to convert their free-falling shares into hard cash which was then stashed away in negligible-interest CDs, treasuries and other non-productive cubbyholes. It was human nature in action — that is to say, Jason Zweig's neurons — demonstrating once again how financial markets react to seemingly different circumstances in a remarkably consistent manner. Whatever crisis you care to examine, they all unfold like the same play performed over and over again, just with different actors.

Central to the real estate disaster was a skyrocketing rate of defaults in sub-prime mortgages, and here the influence of politics stands out in high relief. Home ownership has always been a principal element of the "American Dream," and both parties understand its political appeal. They compete to be recognized as the one best able to help "the little guy" reach the cherished prize — especially if "the little guy" happens to belong to an economic or ethnic group under-represented in home-owner ranks.

Thus recent years have seen efforts, instigated by both Congress and the White House, to encourage home ownership, particularly among low-income voters. For instance, even the "hard-hearted" Bush Administration set a goal of raising home ownership from a sustainable level of 60-62 percent (already a historic peak), up into the high 60s — praiseworthy in a humane sense, perhaps, but somewhat naïve.

And so, through a series of decisions made as a matter of political policy, banks and other lenders were induced to write mortgages a lot of people simply couldn't afford.[7] Now, I blame no one for wanting to own their own home or for wanting to own a *nice* home. I have a nice home, and I appreciate the satisfactions attached to it. In addition, it's certainly true that unrealistic financing occurred among higher-income buyers of upscale houses. The system was distorted from bottom to top.

Why did housing prices collapse? Congress and the policymakers at the Fed are primarily to blame. They created a classic bubble, and bubbles always burst. The Federal Reserve held short-term interest rates too low for too long following the popping of an earlier bubble (the 1990s high-tech/Internet bubble) in 2000. After the stock market slide brought on by the dot-com bust, Alan Greenspan panicked and pushed the Fed Funds Rate down from 6½ percent to 1 percent between July 2000 and July 2003, then kept it there for a full year more. The result was virtually free money, and what was its effect? With money so available and low credit standards (pretty much non-existent, really) by which to obtain it, leverage increased dramatically,

---

7   Everybody is entitled to pursue the "American Dream," and our innate sense of fairness inclines us to wish that people might live in the best way possible. But the reality is that not everyone should own a house. To burden someone with obligations they cannot meet is not social justice; it's debt bondage. There was a time when renting a home was considered perfectly respectable, and under current conditions, that attitude may have to be readopted across the country.

and speculation went wild, especially in housing. Naturally, home prices went up, a lot!

Congress inflated the bubble further. Fannie Mae and Freddie Mac (the Federal National Mortgage Association and the Federal Home Loan Mortgage Corporation) were specifically asked to lower their credit standards when purchasing mortgages from banks and mortgage-backed securities from Wall Street. This came on top of the long-established practice of arm-twisting lenders to make loans with little or no down payments to people with little or no incomes (in the most extreme cases, no jobs) on houses located in areas of questionable prospect.

The combination of loose money and a regulatory atmosphere in which rigor was undone by political expediency aligned all the incentives in the direction of writing mortgages under less than prime conditions (in other words, "sub-prime" mortgages). It was an open invitation for every *shuck-and-jive artist* in the lending industry to snatch easy commissions by hustling the most creative financing to people whose dreams far exceeded their means — and then bundle up these ill-conceived instruments to be dumped on the secondary mortgage market.

There was a good deal of deception in all of this. But it must be said that some of the deception was *self*-deception on the part of borrowers who assumed that growth in their incomes and an endless upward rise in home values would compensate for variable rates.

The flood of bad paper gradually became apparent. But even after George Bush and the Republicans "got religion" and started raising questions about the double-shuffle going on at Fannie and Freddie, the leading congressional enablers of this credit binge did everything they could to block regulatory reform — even urging the two government-sponsored enterprises (GSEs) to take additional risks in the name of "affordable housing."

It's worth noting that, from 2004 to 2006, the most active champions of Fannie and Freddie and their aggressive credit policies were Democrats Barney Frank, Chris Dodd, Chuck Schumer, and oh yes, a new senator from Illinois named Barack Obama. During the same period they were the top four recipients of Fannie and Freddie campaign contributions. What a coincidence!

Some of the nation's most prominent investment houses helped facilitate the housing mania through imaginative packaging and selling of mortgage-backed securities. They were aided in their efforts by rating agencies (the presumed *watchdogs* of the industry) that were curiously incurious about the creditworthiness of these diverse instruments and their underlying debt obligations. Indeed, everyone seems to have had a place at the trough. And it all worked well, as long as housing prices kept going up. But when the residential real estate market — far too overheated — started sputtering in early 2008, a downward spiral began and quickly gathered speed. The result was the worst housing collapse, the worst credit crisis, and worst recession since the 1930s.

Artificial stimulus of the housing market created the bubble, and as is always the case, the enthusiasm of those caught up in it bore little relationship to reality. It was inevitable that the bubble would burst, with prices collapsing of their own weight. But nothing economic occurs in isolation, and the tumbling housing market was no exception. As mortgage default rates went through the roof, causing havoc on balance sheets of financial institutions large and small, both here and around the world, banks failed, credit dried up (for the clean and the unclean alike), and regulators, so recently breezy and lax, turned strict with a vengeance.

Risk Still Matters

The great housing bubble has proven to be an effective object lesson. One of the important points it drives home is the reckless abandon with which some investors were willing to take on risk, even though in the last few years they were very poorly rewarded for the risks they took. As the markets approached historic highs in 2007, financial instruments of all kinds were in such demand by institutional investors that the underlying fundamentals simply couldn't justify much further upward movement. Risk was never eliminated, but it was so widely spread around, "sliced and diced" through the alchemy of derivatives (of which mortgage-backed securities were but one example), that no one knew where it actually resided.

Investors were oblivious to how precarious the whole structure had become — which should have been a red flag that things were about to change. And change they did. In the flight to *quality* in late 2008 and 2009, investors dumped stocks, corporate bonds and mortgage-backed securities to seek shelter in U.S. Treasury securities.

When the world is awash in liquidity, liquidity seems like a given. Some investors foolishly came to view liquidity as a substitute for quality. "If things get bad," they reasoned, "I'll just sell." (But then, who thinks about air when they have no trouble breathing?) Unfortunately, financial markets cannot accommodate everyone trying to exit at the same time. When liquidity dries up, you have many sellers and no buyers.

One of the factors that encouraged sanguine attitudes toward risk in the pre-crash years was the prominence of computer-driven investment strategies promulgated by the megabuck hedge funds. Elaborate models of market behavior, purporting to have microscopically analyzed and infallibly accounted for all variables, provided soothing reassurance to investors. Market forces had become a matter of mathematical projections. Nothing unanticipated could slip past the technological safeguards.

Until the bottom fell out.

Then came the excuses — "Our risk models didn't pick up the fact that we were due for a correction"; "It was the perfect negative storm" — and so many others that it's almost comical to see how far computer models can go off track during a panic. Matthew Rothman, a quantitative analyst for Lehman Brothers, may have put it best when he noted, "Events that models only predicted would happen once in 10,000 years happened every day for three days." One could easily adopt, as the computer modeler's version of *Murphy's Law*, the truism that models tend to fail at the worst possible times, and when they do, they fail spectacularly. Add the effects of financial leverage, and the results can be truly catastrophic.

Given the cheap sources of funding and low-return environment of recent years, it was inevitable that some market participants would use lots of leverage to boost their returns. That works just fine when times are good. But when the unexpected happens and financially stretched investors are forced to sell regardless of price, the effects on markets can be dramatic. In extreme cases, when prices drop too fast, some investors can't sell enough to even remain solvent. A number of hedge funds collapsed in late 2008 for just that reason.

The attraction of modeling is understandable. It's inviting to think that dispassionate technology — unemotional computers with access to unimaginably vast stores of data and virtually limitless capacity with which to manipulate it — can somehow circumvent our human limitations. But this ignores the critical importance of human experience and judgment. It's a heuristic fallacy, and in its way, another expression of herd psychology, only in this case, the herd we follow is a herd of machines. Technology can never be detached from our knowledge, our ignorance, or our biases. Mathematical projections are only as good as the information on which they're based, computers only as good as the people who program them.

Over time, markets have the wonderful ability to sort out the wheat from the chaff, though that sorting process can be difficult. It's important to remember the merits of having a *long-term investment horizon*. Events that dominate the short term recede into nothingness when viewed over an extended time period. As the writer of *Ecclesiastes* reminds us, there really is nothing new under the sun. Likewise, nothing old lasts forever. Three years from now, sub-prime mortgages will be seen only dimly in life's rear-view mirror, just one more panic largely forgotten.

The expansionary monetary policies and massive government spending undertaken by the Obama Administration has helped the housing market recover somewhat from an extremely depressed level. In addition the normal cyclical rise in business activity will increase the demand for housing, sopping up some excess supply. Nevertheless, the enormity of the housing bubble means that recovery will involve a lengthy digestive process. If market forces are allowed to work unhampered by disruptive government policies, supply and demand will set the clearing price for distressed real estate, just as for any other commodity. Unfortunately, re-election cycles for politicians don't accommodate the time which natural market forces require to do their work. Experience tells us to anticipate more tinkering with the tax laws, more efforts to boost the economy, more posturing as champions of "the little guy."

The economic policies of the current administration, are likely to produce a contradictory combination of stimulative monetary policy and contractionary fiscal policy — that is to say, *tax increases* (only on the wealthy, of course, though I expect the definition of "wealthy" to prove extremely elastic). This will lead to higher levels of inflation. So those counting on an extended period of little or no inflation are apt to be disappointed.

chapter 7

Will Common Sense Prevail?

When our current Holy Father, Benedict XVI, was Prefect of the Congregation for the Doctrine of the Faith (as Joseph Cardinal Ratzinger), he delivered a paper at a Rome symposium titled, "Church and Economy in Dialogue." In it he made two critical points that bear on the relationship between finance and morality. To those inclined toward uninformed moral judgments about market economics he warned, "A morality that believes itself able to dispense with the technical knowledge of economic laws is not morality but moralism. As such it is the antithesis of morality." And to those whose predisposition is to separate economic analysis from any sense of moral judgment, he warned, "A scientific approach that believes itself capable of managing without an ethos misunderstands the reality of man. Therefore it is not scientific."

Proper understanding of financial affairs requires a fusion of technical and ethical awareness, insisted the man who would be Pope...

"Today we need a maximum of specialized economic understanding, but also a maximum of ethos so that specialized economic understanding may enter the service of the right goals.

Only in this way will its knowledge be both politically practicable and socially tolerable."[1]

Similarly, one cannot attempt to understand the dynamics of the market — whose proper functioning is so vital to meeting human needs — without considering the forces of politics that impinge upon it. To do so would defy moral logic. So let's delve a bit more deeply into some political ideas and trends that have touched investing concerns.

Reagan vs. Obama

Writing in the foreword to a 2008 book chillingly titled, *The End of Prosperity*, my friend and Catholic Advisory Board member, Larry Kudlow, notes, "An economic model which emphasizes free-market capitalism is the engine of prosperity." As evidence he points to the "Reagan Revolution" which "ushered in 25 years of prosperity, the likes of which has seldom been seen in American or world economic history."

Ronald Reagan argued for monetary control by the Fed to contain inflationary pressure, as the significantly lower tax rates he was able to push through Congress reignited the nation's economic growth in the wake of Carter *stag-flation*. Reagan understood that the capital needed for that growth would flow into the economy only if investors had a reasonable expectation that investing would pay — which is to say, their after-tax gains would be sufficient to make it worth the risk.

"Reagan's supply-side policies took effect quickly and lasted a long time," Kudlow writes, "The U.S. reclaimed the status of economic superpower. Nations around the world imitated the U.S. with success, and literally hundreds of millions of formerly impoverished people

---

1   The pope's paper, "Market Economy and Ethics" by Joseph Cardinal Ratzinger (1985), was originally published in English by *Communio* (Fall 1986). It is available online from The Acton Institute (http://www.acton.org/publications/occasionalpapers/publicat_occasionalpapers_ratzinger.php?view=print).

moved into the middle class around the globe, proving that market capitalism is the greatest anti-poverty program ever devised by man."[2]

In his inspirational book, *The Spirit of Democratic Capitalism*, Michael Novak, another of our Catholic Advisory Board members, pointed out that "capitalism is good, because of all the economic systems devised by man, it is the one that lifts the greatest numbers out of poverty. It is not just an economic system, it is a public good."[3]

How long ago the Reagan era seems these days. After the first year of the era of "Change" it looks like the Administration is hell-bent on undoing the legacy of "The Gipper" as quickly and thoroughly as possible. Ironically, it's being done in the name of "fairness" and a "progressivism" that boasts an exclusive claim on human compassion.

Our current President is a man of many gifts, none the least of which is a gift for verbal communication which has been described as "Reaganesque." But without doubt, his greatest gift is the gift of *misdirection*, that classic technique of magicians for drawing attention elsewhere while performing the slight-of-hand. Obama poses as a defender of markets while erecting elaborate bureaucratic constructions that resemble Reaganomics a whole lot less than they suggest Marxist state control.

A perfect example would be his repeated claims that he had no interest in having the federal government run General Motors. The goal, he insisted, was to give GM an "opportunity" to restructure itself as a "stronger and more competitive company."

What has he *really* done? He's effectively nationalized General Motors Corporation. He fired Rick Wagoner and half the board of directors, put a new CEO in place, and established a government guarantee of the warranties on GM vehicles. He has dictated what kinds of cars will be produced; so-called "green" cars will be given preference over the SUVs and trucks which Americans have shown they actually

---

2　*The End of Prosperity: How Higher Taxes Will Doom the Economy — If We Let It Happen*, by Arthur B. Laffer, Stephen Moore and Peter Tanous, published by Simon & Schuster (2008).

3　*The Spirit of Democratic Capitalism*, by Michael Novak, published jointly by the American Enterprise Institute and Simon & Schuster (1982).

want to buy. Further, Obama's auto team allocated a sizeable equity interest in the new GM to the United Auto Workers, who along with the teachers unions and trial lawyers, helped put Obama in the White House.

All of which doesn't quite jibe with his many denials.

Most Americans are opposed to government managing the auto industry. And of course, that's not what he's doing, Obama insists — not at all, not in the least. Heavens no! Perish the thought! But then, most Americans voted for him, didn't they? When you think about it, Obama's experience with the American electorate doesn't really argue for the importance of candor and transparency. A few head-fakes in the direction of free-market capitalism have served him quite well enough.

And then there's healthcare.

As this is written, Congress has failed to meet Obama's ever-receding series of deadlines for reforming the nation's medical and health-insurance systems. Joe Lieberman, the Senate gadfly who, time and again, proves himself a shining, though ignored, light among the Democrats who have so often rejected him, has urged his colleagues not to rush into health reform. (He wisely insisted that a huge new government commitment whose limits no one can foresee is the last thing we need to take on when we're struggling to climb out of recession.) At the same time, the vigorous townhall protests have given our lawmakers nightmares of tar and feathers.

Such democracy-in-action has prompted Administration trial-balloon comments about how direct federal control of health insurance — the so-called, "government option" — may not be essential to reform, after all, and of course needn't be an obstacle to some kind of meaningful action. But it's pretty obvious that this is more slight-of-hand. Government dominance is the ultimate goal, no matter how circuitous a route Obama must take to lead us there. The lure of controlling an industry that represents about one fifth of America's economy is too close to his heart.

Déjà vu All Over Again

There's much about the campaign for healthcare reform that brings to mind Yogi Berra's famous malapropism, "It's like déjà vu all over again." We have been here before — in 1993, actually, with the Clinton Administration's ill-fated "Hillarycare" initiative. But the Clintons' failed attempt at socializing U.S. medicine offers no assurance that Obama won't succeed. The political stars are aligned quite differently now. Barack Obama is a determined ideologue, he has powerful interests behind him, and even if the Democrats haven't been able to keep all their troops marching in a straight line, they still control the White House and both Houses of Congress (with realignment of the Supreme Court next on the agenda). This fight will go on.

Meanwhile, it's important to remember that, notwithstanding the "Hillarycare" debacle, there has been a steady increase in individuals and segments of the population brought into those aspects of healthcare that are already socialized: Medicare and Medicaid. Recent decades have seen increases in the numbers of welfare recipients, veterans, seniors, children, the uninsured, even illegal immigrants receiving subsidized medical treatments.

A vast, well organized, sophisticated advocacy network, employing Congressional lobbying, civil litigation, street-level agitating, and other less polite tactics, has accomplished the extension of government health services to lengths well beyond Lyndon Johnson's wildest "Great Society" dreams. And this formidable army is now at the disposal of the "Organizer-in-Chief," chomping at the bit to bring health reform to the whole nation. Just how deeply committed to this vision these people are was made plain when the White House quickly pulled down its trial balloons, insisting that the government option was still very much on the table.

Obama has represented the government option as the spark to ignite competition among private companies, making the insurance market more accommodating to families currently unable to obtain adequate coverage, and ultimately bringing down rates for everyone. This argument so thoroughly contradicts market realities — and is so patently disingenuous — that it invites ridicule. Unlike private insurers, a public entity would not be constrained by the need to produce a profit. Subsidized with unlimited federal funds, it would eventually drive all of its private competitors out of business. The result would be "Hillarycare" (in a re-christened form): a single-payer, government-run health insurance system — in other words, socialized medicine.

Far from reducing the costs of healthcare, one of the promised benefits of reform, costs would spiral. The Congressional Budget Office projects a commitment of $1.6 trillion over the next 10 years, but can one be confident in that estimate? Jason Trennert of Strategas Research Partners recently uncovered a bit of historical trivia that gives us cause to wonder. The official actuarial estimate for the 1965 Medicare legislation forecast that total spending would be $9 billion by 1990. Actually it topped $100 billion — off by a factor of 10 (close enough for government work).

At the core of Obama's flawed proposal lies the problem that has bedeviled Medicare and Medicaid. Patients are not sensitive to the costs of medical services. Since they don't pay out of their own pockets, they don't feel the pain of the expenses they generate. Moving all of healthcare insurance to a government single-payer system would raise the problem to a much higher order of magnitude. It's human nature in action again — when people are not responsible for the costs of services they receive, their incentive to be conscious of those costs is negligible and their incentive to take full advantage of whatever is available increases. This is why hospital emergency rooms are already clogged with welfare cases.

Yet, costs would have to be brought under control somehow. Logic dictates that the only way this can be done is by allocating services on a more planned basis, which brings us to the word which the President never utters: *rationing*. The government would limit access to treatments regarded as too expensive or non-economic, making such determinations on a case-by-case basis. It would *have* to. Indeed, the alternative would be gridlock, as all citizens seeking medical assistance would turn to the one and only, government-controlled health system whenever a need arose.

Yet another of our Catholic Advisory Board members, Phyllis Schlafly, has noted that the mechanisms for healthcare rationing are already being put in place...

"The Stimulus provides billions of dollars to an Office of National Coordinator for Health Information Technology to monitor treatments and decide which are cost effective and which will be permitted or denied. Currently, patients make these decisions without government interference. The bottom line is that the Stimulus creates a new system of rationing medical care. This moves healthcare away from the safe and effective standard, and replaces it with what bureaucrats think is cost effective. Obama's 'change' really means government control over access to medical treatments."[4]

The burdens of such rationing would fall heavily on older patients, whose life-expectancy horizons and other age-related factors would argue against heavy investments in expensive treatments. But it's not such a great leap to imagine that similar judgments would be made in cases involving individuals with handicaps or chronic impairments. Quality-of-life questions are already factored into treatment decisions (anybody remember Terri Schiavo?). You can be certain they would loom large to federal bureaucrats charged with medical cost containment — and equally certain that they would be insulated, by law and policy, from the mitigating influence of any religiously-based moral scruples about human dignity and the sanctity of life

Fortunately, the public has expressed considerable skepticism about Obama's plans to revolutionize American healthcare. A recent poll by Resurgent Republic, a non-profit education organization, showed that, by a 60-percent to 31-percent margin, Americans prefer getting their health coverage through private insurance, rather than the Federal government. The same poll showed that 83 percent of

4   *The Phyllis Schlafly Report*, Eagle Forum, July 2009.

Americans are very or somewhat satisfied with the quality of care they and their families currently receive.

It would therefore be fair to say that the vast majority of people are not convinced that across-the-board reforms in the healthcare system are even needed. Further, it's absurd for President Obama to claim that a government healthcare system could control costs better than the market-based system. The history of Medicare negates that assertion. A recent study by the Pacific Research Institute found that since 1970, Medicare costs have risen 34 percent per year faster than healthcare costs generally.

And then there's *Cap and Trade.*

The *Wall Street Journal* recently ran an editorial called, "The Cap and Trade Fiction," which adroitly pointed out that, to get Cap and Trade through Congress, the Democrats would have to "destroy the discipline of economics."

The Cap and Trade bill — which might better be called the "Kill the Economy" bill — is supposed to reduce emissions of the "greenhouse gases" (mostly CO_2) that allegedly contribute to the "global warming" that is allegedly changing the Earth's climate. Now, whether or not one believes in global warming really isn't the issue, and I won't go into it (except to note that, in the 1970s, some climatologists were warning of an impending ice age). The relevant point is that, as proposed by the Obama Administration, Cap and Trade would be one of the most economically debilitating schemes ever conceived.

The idea would be to set caps on carbon emissions by industry sector, granting permits that would allow companies to discharge effluent gasses up to the prescribed limits. Since some companies would exceed their limits while others wouldn't use their entire allotted capacity, the permits could be traded on an open market, with the net effect that overall emissions would stay within desired total bounds. Supporters of this proposition argue that the system would be a boon to the economy. Forcing companies to trim energy consumption and costs would spur entire new technologies and "green" industries — which is rather like saying that being hit by a hurricane is good for the economy of a town because the locals get to build new houses.[5]

To see the actual effects of such an effort, we have only to look "across the pond" at our British cousins. The United Kingdom has attempted to cut its carbon emissions for several years now, and the British Taxpayer Alliance estimates that the average family there currently pays approximately $1,300 a year in "green" taxes (over and above other national and local tax obligations). If the Democrats are able to push through the Cap and Trade bill, they will have laid a gigantic tax increase on Americans of all income brackets — contradicting candidate Obama's well remembered pledge that "taxpayers earning less than $250,000 a year will not see their taxes increased by even one dime."

Once again to our good fortune, as with healthcare reform, public skepticism is on the rise. As both voters and politicians come to see that the case for climate change isn't exactly cut and dried, and as they begin to grasp the dangers posed by efforts to combat it, the enthusiasm for Cap and Trade is waning.

Obama presents himself as a deficit cutter, while he's expanding the deficit at an unimaginable pace and stifling free markets in the process. He claims his stimulus program is designed to spark growth in energy, healthcare, education, and other areas. What I see growing is the influence of unions — disrupters of free markets by their very nature — which represents a sharply leftward turn in the relationship between government and the economy, and is the exact opposite of growth promotion.

I feel my views vindicated by the CBO, which recently projected a deficit in excess of $9 trillion over the next ten years if Obama's program should be put into place. This would *triple* the national debt, the consequences of which would be dire.

---

5   There are provisions in the Cap and Trade bill that touch families, too. It is estimated that homeowners would face increased energy costs of up to $175 per year, along with numerous regulations mandating construction features and materials that would raise the cost of any home being sold — not an appealing prospect in the current real estate market.

Obama's ambitions are endless. His ultimate desire seems to be to remake the U.S. economy according to the pattern of European Social Democracy, a pattern that features heavily unionized work-forces, low productivity, stagnant economic growth, consequent high unemployment, and a net outflow of people. As one sage put it, "The problem with socialism is that you eventually run out of other people's money."[6]

However, one of the reasons the stock market staged a 50-percent recovery in only six months, after bottoming out March 9, 2009, was because of investor recognition that most of Obama's plans were not likely to be implemented, at least not to the extent he envisioned. His appetite for *change* is simply too big, and increasingly, the public is realizing that his "change you can believe in" is really change for the worse.

The Continuing Threat

The recession has had one ironic, though salutary, effect: it helped to dampen inflation. As the recovery continues, it must be recognized that the inflation threat persists. Elected officials may decry inflation's evils, but somehow they don't seem able to avoid the policies and practices that bring it on. Moreover, there's a case to be made that people actually *like* inflation. They want CDs with high interest rates and the enriching sensation derived from watching the nominal value of homes appreciate. They enjoy being able to pay back loans with money that's worth less than when they borrowed it (a reality from which governments also benefit).

For all the good it may do stock and bond prices, *low* inflation really doesn't have much of a constituency. And as of the end of 2009, with the rate reduced to near zero, inflation isn't an issue of great con-

---

6   This pithy insight is attributed to former British Prime Minister Margaret Thatcher —
    though other clear thinkers could lay claim to alternate versions, many predating her com-
    ment. Whoever said it first, it remains one of those durable truths that continue to under-
    mine the elaborate schemes of leftward politicians so concerned with the interests of "the
    little guy."

cern one way or the other. Consequently, I'm afraid that neither the Administration nor the Fed will muster the discipline necessary to contain inflation once it shows itself again. Rather, when confronted with the consequences of their economic policies, they will likely embrace it as a way out of their problems. They'll turn on the printing presses and let 'em roll, an easy short-term remedy that always has negative long-term consequences.

Inflation is an outgrowth of the political process. It is cyclical in nature, and right now, we're at or near the low point in its cycle. Even while it may seem like inflation is dead, several warning signs say otherwise. Hard assets (commodities) have significantly outperformed financial assets for the past decade. Copper, silver, lumber, oil, gold and coffee prices have surged recently. Many economists believe it's primarily fear of future inflation and a weak dollar that's driving investors and commodity users to push up prices. If so, the monetary policies pursued by the Fed — massive creation of money — fuel that fear.

The Commodities Research Bureau's Futures Index is up 17 percent just since February 2009, led by grains, precious metals, industrial raw materials, and energy. Similarly, the *Journal of Commerce* index of raw materials is way above the level of a year ago. While the Consumer Price Index (CPI) has remained almost flat over the past 12 months, forward-looking commodity prices are telling a different story: resurgent inflation, because rising commodity prices are an early indicator.

My favorite economist of all time, Milton Friedman, referred to the monetary base (loans made and securities purchased by the Fed) as "high-powered money." Monetarists believe the rate of change in high-powered money is the main determinant of economic activity. When it accelerates more rapidly than real goods and services are created, you get inflation. High-powered money has been expanded at a 100-percent annual rate in 2008 and 2009, implying a high likelihood of escalation in the rate of inflation.

U.S. capacity utilization, a commonly quoted indicator of economic activity, is currently only 65 percent, and wage inflation is non-existent. Therefore, near-term, the CPI is not about to explode upward. But unless the Fed can drain excess liquidity from the system, when the economy starts to recover, inflation will be back *big-time!*

All of this is exacerbated by current fiscal policies. The term "deficit spending" seems inadequate to describe how the government is burning through money at a level far beyond the revenue it collects. And with Obama's limitless visions of reform — in healthcare, energy policy, education, the financial system, and so much more — to be accomplished through mammoth additional spending programs, inflationary pressure will be magnified many times over.

I am not making a hard and fast prediction that we will return to the double-digit inflation of the late 1970s. But the country *is* faced with resurgent cyclical inflation, which may well be above 5 percent by 2011. And more likely than not, prices will continue rising for a longer period than most observers now expect. Once it gets rolling, inflation has the unpleasant characteristic of running further than measured analysis would seem to indicate. Accordingly, wise investors are rearranging their portfolios to include hard assets and commodities, such as gold, silver, oil and other natural resource-related investments as an insurance policy (which, as with any insurance, we should hope is not needed).[7]

For the moment, the issue is *de-*flation. The massive credit contraction and the de-leveraging of American society and its financial institutions, while much needed, are having the effect of deflating numerous industries and the economy in general. So the CPI is not in any near-term danger of escalating. But if the great liberal juggernaut cannot be stopped, it'll be *"Katie, bar the door!"* when the economy does recover.

---

7 Another sign of investor preparations for inflation is the growing popularity of TIPS (Treasury Inflation-Protected Securities), a type of U.S. Treasury bond that offers some protection against inflation by making adjustments to principal.

    While TIPS are useful for stashing cash, they don't come close to equities as long-term investments. Still, they have their place. Further information about TIPS and how to acquire them can be obtained online at: http://www.treasurydirect.gov/indiv/products/prod_tips_glance.htm.

I am hopeful that the Tea Parties, which spread like wild fire around the country, will have an impact. I pray it works out that way — that the enormous benefits derived from the Reagan revolution will not be reversed, and Americans will not suffer from the socialist policies of the current administration. Obama's policies so far are exactly opposite of the successful Reagan policies. Obama wants to *raise* taxes, increase spending and weaken the dollar.

These profligate tax and spending initiatives combined with the near zero-percent interest rate policy of the Federal Reserve almost guarantee a high level of inflation down the road. Governments never openly promote inflation, but because it allows them to pay off debt with cheaper dollars, they tolerate it. Our Federal government seems well prepared to do so. Inflation can provide short-term relief and fool people into thinking things are getting better. But it hurts real growth, it hurts savers, and it hurts productivity.

I'm of the view that fooling people is what the Obama administration is all about. Obama is the consummate con man, saying one thing and doing the exact opposite. Before his term of office (hopefully only one term) is over, people will be quoting what Abraham Lincoln had to say about fakers: "You can fool some of the people all the time, and you can fool all of the people some of the time, but you can't fool all of the people all of the time."

The question now is: How will prosperity return? There is only one answer: the encouragement of business through modest taxation, sound monetary and fiscal policy, restrained government, and creation of an economic climate in which business owners can expect to earn a reasonable profit for the risks they take. The factor that is most harmful to business confidence is *uncertainty*, and in its first year, the Obama Administration has made uncertainty a veritable keynote.

Good Sense Persists

I do not think the U.S. will be foolish enough to go very far down the socialist path. I do not *think* so. Because our country is still a capitalist nation, and economic reality is a strong corrective even for the most callow, idealistic nonsense.

While Americans have always been extraordinarily charitable toward those less fortunate, and ready to pull together in times of war and great national stress, the principle at the heart of our society is *individualism*. We consider all our fellow citizens as equal before the law, but we cherish the notion that anyone can go as far as talent, effort and good luck will allow — which implies a high degree of tolerance for inequality of outcomes. This aspect of our national character is something which foreigners who have never experienced life in the U.S. find very hard to grasp. And it's what has — up to this point — restricted the appeal of socialism. People shy away from imposing egalitarian limits on the heights to which they might aspire.

But despite the distinctiveness of our outlook and the history that has given it its shape, human nature has not been overcome. We may desire the widest latitude for fulfillment of our self-interest, but we are as susceptible as any people to the lure of *the easy way*. The great French Catholic political thinker, Alexis de Tocqueville, observed this on his tour of our young nation during the 1830s. In his masterwork, *Democracy In America*, he recorded: "The American Republic will endure until the day Congress discovers that it can bribe the public with the public's money."[8]

By now, Congress — with both houses firmly in the hands of the Democrats — and of course, the White House, have indeed discovered this sad fact. The effort to bring Tocqueville's prophecy to fruition is well underway. My hope is that the working of the free market economy will defeat such plans. Because losing America's great vision of individual liberty, opportunity and accomplishment would not only be a historic defeat, it would be a moral disaster. Deprivation would triumph; people would suffer; freedom would be curtailed.

We have seen it happen before, many times. The young survey respondents who shared their fondness for socialism with those Rasmussen pollsters really should view some old photos of bedraggled and frustrated Russian shoppers queued up — often for days — out-

---

8 *Democracy In America*, by Alexis-Charles-Henri Clérel de Tocqueville (1805-1859), published in two volumes, 1835 and 1840.

side empty Soviet stores. And those lines were only the visible signs of much more profound and debilitating restrictions on individual liberty and aspiration.

I am convinced that God does not wish such an outcome for the United States, as He does not wish it for any country. Instead, I believe with Ronald Reagan, that it remains America's destiny to serve as a beacon to the world, a "shining city on a hill." And with that faith, I trust in capitalism to prevail.

chapter 8

Investment Planning

"Investing is most intelligent when it is business-like." Warren Buffett has called that observation, penned by his mentor, Benjamin Graham, the "nine most important words ever written about investing."

No doubt, there are professional gamblers who would insist that they evaluate risk, assess their ratio of wins to losses, and adjust tactical procedures in ways that approximate business. But gambling generally presents only restricted choices. Opportunities for planning, adaptivity, or the application of knowledge and skill tend to be closely circumscribed. Randomness and chance are the predominant elements in most forms of gaming, boldness a gambler's most efficacious personal quality.

With investments, on the other hand, a rational, orderly, businesslike approach balancing initiative and prudence, and maintained over an extended period of time, is what's most likely to yield positive results. That's why investing is different from gambling. And when your motives for investing include religious or moral intentions, the demands of stewardship make being business-like an ethical imperative.

I have approached the development of the Ave Maria Mutual Funds in a highly business-like manner. I've spent years extolling the virtues of *asset allocation*, that is, of diversifying one's portfolio with different investment styles. So it was apparent to me from the start that our Catholic Values Fund was likely to be the first in a *family* of funds. After all, how could we claim it was possible for investors to meet their financial goals in a morally responsible way, unless we were prepared to offer them a broad array of investment options.

Our shareholders were thinking along similar lines, and early on, we began to receive inquiries about when we could offer other funds to meet investment styles and objectives not covered by the Catholic Values Fund.

Why Diversification?

Diversification of investments is generally recognized as an essential means of mitigating risk and maximizing returns over the long term. By allocating your investments over different asset classes and styles, you'll reduce risk and increase your probability of gain over a complete market cycle.

The same principle holds if all your investing is done through mutual funds. The Investment Company Institute (the trade association for mutual funds) lists over 8,000 member funds covering different investment styles and tailored to a wide variety of investment objectives. There are stock funds specializing in certain industries, focusing on specific companies according to size, sales volume, growth potential, geographic coverage, and other characteristics. There are bond funds, commodity funds, real estate funds, foreign funds, and money-market funds. There are funds whose objective is rapid growth, as opposed to funds whose holdings concentrate solely on the icons of industry, the well known *blue chips* that dominate the global business scene. Then there are funds that seek out emerging companies, the *small caps* that have hopes of becoming business giants. And of course, there are the *go anywhere* funds that mix stocks and bonds with commodities, currency and pretty much anything else (like the Magellan Fund, once run by the legendary fund manager, Peter Lynch).

The multiplicity of funds available is virtually endless, with all this variety aimed at giving investors maximum choice. To be sure, it's also designed to provide brokers and financial planners with different kinds of financial products to offer. In fact, there are plenty of mutual funds which seem to have little rationale for their existence beyond marketing appeal. The financial services industry is as prone to novelty (or, if you prefer, to *gimmickry*) as any other business oriented to sales. And let the buyer beware — just because a fund is offered by a reputable brokerage firm, there's no guarantee that it particularly makes sense.

Two obvious advantages of investing in mutual funds are instant diversification and professional management. You can never be absolutely certain that a given fund is going to be a winner, but at least you know that someone is managing the portfolio. Professional fund managers provide a level of attentive oversight and sophisticated capabilities for stock analysis and selection which most individual investors don't have the time or expertise to provide for themselves — though to be sure, not all fund managers are equally talented or focused on their task.

The key difference between mutual funds and investing in individual stocks is *consistency*. As Jason Zweig's observations of investor behavior so clearly demonstrate, emotion tends to override intention. People jump into or out of particular stocks impetuously, often on very little tangible information. They're easily excited by companies that "look good," or they panic at the first hint of a setback. Overall, they assume too much about their ability to outguess the market. All of which contributes to highly erratic investing behavior and consequent disappointing results.

Professional managers, on the other hand, may be no less human in their emotional makeup, but they usually have a longer-term perspective — especially those with a solid grounding in the Value Investing approach. And day-in/day-out market experience fosters a certain clinical detachment that can help keep emotions under control. Aside from those "lemmings" whom I decry as being subject to the Wall Street herd mentality, I generally have great respect for my mutual fund-manager colleagues. I'll admit to having known some fund managers with poor professional skills and volatile emotions. But as a general principle, I put my money on the pros.

Perhaps the most self-defeating investment foible is jumping in and out of different mutual funds. Investors bitten by the market-timing bug too often figure that if they can keep ahead of individual stocks, they can do the same with funds. In actuality, they rarely do very well with either. In the case of funds, the numbers tell a sad and indisputable story. From 1926 through 2008, the average yearly return on equity mutual funds was 10 percent, while returns to investors who held shares in those funds, at one time or another, came in at only slightly above 3 percent.[1] This is a noteworthy contrast. It demonstrates the destructive effects of inconsistency, the negative impact of emotionalism, and the importance of patience.

Just as with most people who invest in individual stocks, too many mutual fund investors react emotionally in contradiction of common sense. They tend to buy when they're feeling confident — which is to say, after prices have already risen — and they tend to sell when their confidence is shaken by falling prices. In other words, they buy *high* and sell *low*. What you really want to do is buy solid, well managed funds that meet your investment objectives and then stick with them.

Whatever the composition of your investment portfolio, every now and then it may be necessary to make some adjustments, in order to rebalance the allocation of assets you've determined is right for you (say, 60 percent stocks to 40 percent bonds, or whatever ratios you've set). Also, you occasionally might want to sell something to free up cash so you can take advantage of another opportunity. Conditions evolve, and flexibility is a virtue. But whether you're dealing with mutual funds or individual securities (or both), don't go redesigning your investment strategy with every jiggle in the market. That's a formula for definite and sustained failure.

Expanded Offerings

With the success of the Ave Maria Catholic Values Fund, our shareholders were convinced that Morally Responsible Investing could work. Lingering worries that the constraints imposed on our screening

---

1   Figures obtained from the Investment Company Institute.

process might be too restrictive were set aside, and there was a high degree of satisfaction with our Value Investing approach.[2] Now the question was: When would we apply the MRI concept to other investment styles, in particular to bonds and growth-type stocks? We began exploring how to design other funds in a morally responsible way.

As far as growth was concerned, it wasn't all that easy. In the years following the '90s "dot-com" frenzy, it often appeared that the most promising companies were the hip, free-wheeling, entrepreneurial high-tech enterprises — the Apples, Microsofts and Googles of the world — that had emerged from the rubble of the so-called "New Economy." These outfits were innovative, their products were exciting, and they had proven themselves to be survivors. But many of them were way over the horizon of moral sympathies from MRI. We encountered corporate policies that were aggressive in their support of Planned Parenthood, actively campaigned for candidates and legislation of highly dubious moral prospect, and much else that put them out of bounds for us.

But we weren't discouraged. Research uncovered plenty of companies with the investment characteristics and sound balance sheets we were looking for — corporations whose policies and practices didn't violate the core principles of the Catholic Church. So, on May 1, 2003, two years after the May Day on which we had launched the Catholic Values Fund, the Ave Maria Growth Fund went live, side-by-side with the Ave Maria Bond Fund, which we had been developing simultaneously.

Launching new funds on the day dedicated to our Patroness has become something of a tradition. The Rising Dividend Fund premiered on May 1, 2005, the Opportunity Fund on May 1, 2006, and the Ave Maria Money Market Account on May 1, 2007. The menu of funds we have created provides a considerable amount of diversifica-

---

2 Some restrictions included in the screening process would present us with a surprising situation in the future, and adjustments would be made. I'll address that later.

tion possibilities, which is essential to developing a comprehensive investment strategy.[3]

The Ave Maria Money Market Account, itself, represents a certain diversification in our professional practices. It's a joint venture with Federated Securities, Inc., the Pittsburgh-based company that virtually created money market funds. I had long been aware of Federated. Back in the mid-1970s, when I was managing the trust investments of National Bank and Trust Company of Ann Arbor, I was visited by Glen Johnson, a Federated salesman (he would later become the company's president). Johnson wanted to acquaint me with the money market fund concept, a relatively new idea at the time. I thought it might be something useful to offer our trust customers — mainly as a way to park money, pending a more permanent investment — so I signed up.

Useful as they are, I have never really thought of money market funds as investment vehicles. But from the standpoint of good mutual fund management, their effectiveness in gathering assets is obvious. Federated currently has assets under management in excess of $400 billion. It's been positively dazzling to observe how money market funds have become such prominent fixtures on the financial scene. And since a lot of our shareholders were interested in adding some sort of cash component to their portfolios, we decided to explore creating a money market fund of our own.

In late 2006, I had the opportunity to meet Jack Donahue, Federated's founder and chairman, at the annual meeting of Legatus, the Catholic business leaders group Tom Monaghan started. Seated together with our wives at dinner, I told him about my interest in starting a money market fund.

"Good luck!" he said in a tone that was distinctly not encouraging.

When I pressed him, he explained some of the complications involved in pulling off what I had in mind. Starting such a fund would

---

3   We currently don't offer an international fund. However, many of the companies whose shares are held by the funds in the Ave Maria family have significant international operations, even if they are headquartered here in the good old USA.

be extremely hard, he said, and the details he shared were convincing (as a pioneer of the industry, he was the man to know[4]). His comments also paralleled what we had already begun to find out through our explorations into the mechanics and logistics of money market funds.

I was pleased to discover that Jack Donahue was familiar with the Ave Maria Mutual Funds and what we had accomplished so far. Then I was pretty much *floored* when he suggested undertaking a joint venture with Federated. I told him I would be delighted to consider such an option, and soon after, one of his senior executives, Amy Michaliszyn, came to our offices in Michigan to make a presentation to the Schwartz Investment Trust Board of Trustees.

The relationship we've established with Federated has been most gratifying. The Ave Maria Money Market Account has become popular with our shareholders, currently topping more than $25 million in assets. Federated handles all management, basically as an extension of its $1 billion-plus Automated Government Cash Reserves Fund. The operation passes muster from a Morally Responsible Investing point of view, because it buys only short-term money market instruments of the U.S. Treasury and U.S. agency obligations — and doesn't include securities of Fannie Mae and Freddie Mac, both of which contribute to Planned Parenthood. Staying away from Fannie and Freddie has also shielded us from the anxieties associated with the mortgage-backed securities mess.

Interestingly, recent developments have served to strengthen the security of money market funds. In late 2008, when the financial crisis was at its most fevered, a money market fund called the Reserve Fund (no connection with Federated) "broke the buck," meaning it found itself with insufficient funds to repay its investors $1.00 for each dollar they'd put in. It seems the fund had large holdings of Lehman Brothers commercial paper, and when Lehman went down, that paper became worthless. The Reserve Fund could pay only $.91 on the dol-

---

4   The fascinating story of Federated Securities is told in the book, *The Eagle Soars*, published internally by Federated in 1997.

lar, creating panic among investors with cash in money market funds around the country. They rushed to pull out their money as fast as they could. The government stepped in, guaranteeing money market funds for the first time.[5]

Diversification in Funds

Asset allocation applies to mutual funds in exactly the same way as to stocks and bonds. The aim is to spread risk over a variety of securities. That's why I saw the need to build a fund family that offers options geared toward different investing styles and objectives.

The Ave Maria Growth Fund focuses primarily on stocks of high-quality growing enterprises, mostly mid-cap (medium-capitalization) companies. As of Fall 2009, it had a five-star rating from Morningstar, which puts it in the top ten percent of mutual funds in its class. It was conceived as a natural complement to (and introduced simultaneously with) the Ave Maria Bond Fund, a four-star-rated fund (as of Fall 2009) holding short- and intermediate-maturity, investment-grade bonds, and designed to provide steady income with protection of principal.

The other two funds in our family demonstrate a contrast between investing styles. The Ave Maria Rising Dividend Fund is based on companies with medium and large capitalization that are well managed, have recognized proprietary products with strong market positions maintained over time, resulting in long histories of increasing sales, earnings and dividends. Typically, these companies have demonstrated consistently high returns on shareholder equity and above-average profit margins. Also rated five stars, (as of Fall 2009) the Rising Dividend Fund, embodies the Value Investing concept approached in a conservative way.

The Ave Maria Opportunity Fund, on the other hand, is the most aggressive of our offerings, containing companies of all sizes, including

5   The crisis was not without negative consequences for some firms; a number of money market funds closed down. But it worked to the benefit of Federated Securities. One firm, Putnam Funds, decided to get out of the money market business, and turned over its money market fund to Federated — *gratis* — an example of *survival of the fittest*.

small and micro-cap stocks with high appreciation potential. It would be inaccurate to apply the word "speculative" to any Ave Maria fund. My staff and I are not adrenaline junkies; indeed we're the farthest thing from reckless. But, the Opportunity Fund clearly does have a risk component that reflects the high appreciation potential of its component stocks. As with all of our equity funds, we're looking for stocks that are inefficiently priced.

Within the context of Value Investing, the issues we select for the Opportunity Fund are often less seasoned. They may have briefer track records than those included in our other funds. Consequently, they tend to be under-followed by Wall Street analysts and under-owned by institutional investors, so their price-appreciation potential can be greater as they become discovered. The Opportunity Fund, four-star rated by Morningstar as of Fall 2009, is most suited to investors with a tolerance for risk and an extended time horizon. We expect that, over the next few years, it could produce compound average annual rates of return higher than our other Ave Maria Funds, but with more variability of returns.

This six-fund mix demonstrates how the Ave Maria Mutual Fund family achieves broad diversification. And of course, diversification exists within each funds itself. A mutual fund, by its very nature, is an amalgam of investments, so even a single fund offers a significant measure of diversity, which can be increased or decreased according to how the fund is constructed and managed. For instance, we've structured the Ave Maria Bond Fund so that as much as 20 percent of its holdings can be dividend-paying stocks.[6] Those aren't bonds, to be sure, but their presence adds a degree of appreciation potential to what otherwise would be primarily a principal-preservation fund.

With all stocks and bonds in our various funds subject to rigorous moral screening, it is entirely possible to achieve significant diversifica-

6   In many cases, these are equities included in the Rising Dividend Fund: high-quality companies with long histories of increasing dividends. I'm confident that including such stocks will continue to permit the Ave Maria Bond Fund to outperform other funds in its class.

tion while investing exclusively in mutual funds that are faithful to the principles of Morally Responsible Investing.

Researching Mutual Funds

I should offer a few basic thoughts about choosing mutual funds in general. With roughly 8,000 U.S. funds in existence, how can you identify a good one?

Many people haven't a clue about how to judge a mutual fund. They depend on stockbrokers who charge commissions for their advice and, naturally, tend to direct their customers to load funds that generate broker commissions. This is unfortunate and unnecessary. It has been my experience that most investors who are willing to take the time and who have even a rudimentary understanding of investment principles (and a basic level of common sense) are perfectly able to identify good mutual funds for themselves. They can buy no-load funds, and build a comprehensive, diversified and appropriately balanced portfolio of funds, while paying no commissions at all.

In our digital age, much of the information you need is little more than a mouse click away. Investment research sites, such as Morningstar.com, provide a cornucopia of data on virtually every mutual fund in existence, including history, ranking and investment performance, along with background on the people who manage the funds, and lots of other pertinent insight. All this knowledge can be brought right to your computer screen, but it's important to have some sense of what you need to find out.

The first thing to determine when considering a mutual fund is its investment objective — long-term growth? income? capital appreciation? preservation of principal? What has the fund been designed to do, and how does that match up with your own investing goals? Naturally, the kinds of securities a fund holds will correspond to its objectives. Equity funds are made up of stocks; fixed-income funds hold bonds; balanced funds blend both stocks and bonds in varying proportions.

Among equity funds, they are categorized according to whether they are oriented to *growth, value,* or a mix of the two. They are also defined by the level of capitalization of the companies whose stocks they include (large, mid or small). Morningstar uses a nifty little style box to categorize the equity funds they rate: a nine-box matrix that groups funds according to investment style and capitalization. The characteristics of funds you choose should reflect your own investment goals, at least for that portion of your overall portfolio.

Morningstar Equity Fund Matrix[7]

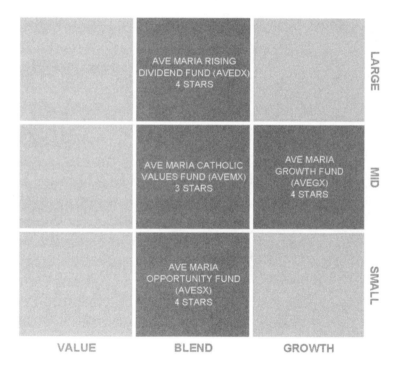

7   Equity fund descriptive matrix - This version shows Morningstar's classifications of the four Ave Maria equity funds. Morningstar ratings as of 12-31-2009. See Appendix C for more information.

Regarding fixed-income (bond) funds, the primary distinction is between investment grade and non-investment grade ("junk") corporate bonds. I have always maintained that most investors should limit their fixed-income investing to investment-grade issues, (that is, no junk). Standard and Poor's ranks investment-grade bonds: AAA; AA; A; and BBB. These are its top four categories. My advice is to stay away from anything below those four. If you don't, you'll probably regret it.

I have always had a very strong preference for simplicity in selecting mutual funds. Most investors should shy away from the complex investment instruments developed in recent decades: *derivatives*[8], *futures contracts, short-selling, credit default swaps* (which brought down AIG), *collateralized debt obligations, IOs, POs,* and the many other arcane devices that give the financial markets an exotic and threatening aura rather like that of an ancient Gnostic cult.

These obscure and flimsy constructions have done little more than invite gamblers eager to speculate on the ups and downs of the market. For instance, there are several speculative leveraged funds that bet on near-term swings in specific industries. Such funds have undermined investment prudence, with often disastrous consequences for unsuspecting investors (speculators). It is exactly such investment "creativity," involving sub-prime mortgages, that helped to lay low some of the nation's most prominent financial institutions.

Instead, I go for plain vanilla. As a Value Investor, I favor funds and stocks that will likely appreciate over the long term. I have always advised people to invest in funds that are broadly diversified over several industry sectors (as all the Ave Maria Mutual Funds are), with no big bets in any one industry or stock. I don't buy derivatives, mortgages or asset-backed securities or sell short (hoping for a decline in the price of a particular stock) in any of the Ave Maria Mutual Funds.

To get a complete view of any fund, it's a good idea to read through the *Prospectus* and *Statement of Additional Information.* These documents, available from the fund's marketing department, and often online as well, are not what you'd call bedtime reading. But they con-

---

8   Buffett refers to derivatives as "instruments of mass destructions."

tain enormous amounts of relevant and useful facts, and you should steel yourself to go through them, intimidating as they may appear.

Pay particular attention to what they say about the portfolio manager and key staff members involved in the investment decision-making process. Are they experienced professionals whose careers have spanned several market cycles, or does the fund appear to have a penchant for younger types? During past "go-go" eras, the young, aggressive risk-takers who managed the hottest funds got all the headlines. But when the inevitable bear markets returned, you didn't hear much about those former hotshots anymore. They usually got fired.

My own bias — evident in the composition of my staff — has always been toward caution and experience, whatever the prevailing market conditions. I take to heart Warren Buffett's humorous observation: "You only have to know two things about investing: Number 1 — don't lose money. And number two — don't forget Number 1."

The most fundamental truth about assessing mutual funds is that there are no magic formulas. A fund is as good as the people who run it, and their track record is on display for all to see. The facts you need to choose funds wisely are available to you. Make the effort to discern them. With a bit of effort and diligence, you can make sound judgments about mutual funds for yourself.

Surviving Tough Times

By the time this book appears, we will have some pretty clear indications of how effective the Obama Administration's stimulus and recovery efforts have been in bringing the country through its financial trials. In the first year of this presidency President Obama has not hewn to the centrist policies his campaign promised. To the contrary, his initiatives display troubling socialist inclinations.

Let's explore the challenge of economic survival if things haven't gone well.

Consider a scenario where loose credit, a flood of government spending, increased taxes, and a bloated deficit bring on a period of higher inflation (say at least 5 percent by mid-2011). What can you do *now* to prepare for such a situation? I'm currently advising my clients to fortify their portfolios with some assets that are a traditional store of value during periods of anticipated inflation. I recommend a modest commitment to gold.

There's a certain awkwardness in advising people to buy gold. The debate over whether it was wise to abandon the gold standard has raged ever since the valuation of currency was detached from the nation's precious-metal holdings. Those who advocate doing away with the Federal Reserve, abrogating all international currency agreements, and restoring specie-backed money are tagged as "gold bugs," and their arguments are often dismissed as totally anachronistic in an age of sophisticated global finance.

No question their prescription would represent an extreme reversal of the nation's historical path, but their attachment to gold is well founded. The ups and downs of economic life demonstrate the undisputable need for some universally recognized standard of value, and throughout history, gold has filled that critical role. Let me make a simple point: from the perspective of prudent investing, gold should not be viewed as an investment, but rather as insurance.

Recently I advised a friend to add some gold to his portfolio. He laughed at me. "I don't want to get involved with gold," he said. "It'll probably just go down in price."

I nodded. "Well, you should hope that it does."

At which point he looked at me quite incredulously. "Why would I want to buy something that's going to drop in price?"

"Do you have fire insurance on your house?" I asked him.

"Of course I have fire insurance. I've had it for years."

"In all those years," I asked, "has your house ever burned down?"

"No."

"Then I guess all the money you spent on insurance premiums has been a waste."

He was really confused by now. "No, it wasn't a waste," he insisted. "It bought me protection, in case I did have a fire."

"Exactly," I said. "And that's what having gold does for your investment portfolio. It buys you protection. If gold goes down, that means your other investments are going up. But if everything else goes down, because of some economic calamity, the price of gold will likely rise. It's a hedge. It will offset other losses. And *that* is the point of owning gold."

Economic stability, low levels of inflation, high corporate profits, and rising stock prices invariably depress the price of gold. But those are *good* things — things investors want to happen — though experience shows that they don't happen consistently. So putting, say, 5 percent of your assets into gold, and thinking of it as an economic insurance policy, is a prudent thing to do. Like insurance, you hope you never need it. But if you do need it, you'll be glad you have it.

We've added gold to several of our Ave Maria Mutual Fund portfolios. We don't trade in physical gold —bullion, coins or jewelry — but rather, we buy shares in an ETF (exchange-traded fund) called SPDR Gold Shares (trading symbol: GLD). This is the largest ETF that tracks the price of gold. It's a gold trust that holds bullion in a depository and reflects the market price, less the trust's expenses, which are quite moderate. Shares are traded daily on the New York Stock Exchange, and are highly liquid. In my view, it's the cheapest and most efficient way to own gold.

Another hedge against inflation is oil. The Ave Maria Mutual Funds have bought significant blocks of several well-run oil companies: Exxon, Forest Oil, Frontier Oil, Halliburton, Schlumberger, XTO Energy, and others that pass our moral screens. After the stunning crude-oil price height of $147 a barrel in mid 2008, oil had dropped to $32 a barrel by early 2009, reflecting the worldwide economic contraction and decreased fuel demand. It then more than doubled off that low by late in the year. I anticipate that, over the next couple of years, as the economy recovers and inflation once again rears its ugly head, oil will lead the upturn in commodity prices. High-quality companies involved in energy production will be the primary beneficiaries of rising prices, and their profit gains will be significant (unless the Obama Administration crushes them with taxes).

Retirement Planning

Age affects everything. It correlates closely with income, and it signals the level of risk you can afford to tolerate in your investments by determining the amount of time you have to accumulate assets or recover from losses. When I started in the investment profession some 40 years ago, it was traditional wisdom to advise clients approaching 65 (the common retirement age) to sell most of their stock holdings and go into fixed-income securities in order to live off the income. In the years since, both life-span assumptions and career expectations have changed markedly, along with a variety of other social factors. Members of the Baby Boom generation (of which I was born on the leading edge) have taken to heart the words of poet, Dylan Thomas, and are not going "gentle" into the "good night" of a brief retirement and rapid decline.

Nowadays, when people turn 65, they could have 30 or more years to live — years for which bond interest alone may not be adequate provision. Consequently, my advice is to keep a healthy portion of assets invested in stocks even after retirement, moving small amounts into higher-yield, fixed-income securities (such as investment-grade bonds), as needed.

During the severely depressed market of early 2009, this was a challenge. Watching stock prices tumble always creates pressure to seek stability, even though this tends to lock in losses and limit recovery potential — a short-term fix that can have damaging long-term financial consequences. "Rage, rage" as we may "against the dying of the light,"[9] time marches on. We get old. In fact, most of us will be old for longer than our parents were. Add to that the increasing anxieties about being able to count on the so-called safety net of Social Security, and the need for greater care in retirement planning becomes obvious.

Almost nothing works as well in accumulating retirement savings as tax-deferred plans (401ks, IRAs, defined-contribution pension

---

9   "Do not go gentle into that good night; Old age should burn and rave at close of day; Rage, rage against the dying of the light...." — from Dylan Thomas' poem, "Do Not Go Gentle Into that Good Night."

funds, and others). The ability to stockpile assets without paying 15 to 35 percent in yearly taxes means your investments can compound at a higher rate, giving you the potential to accumulate substantially more money to carry you beyond your working years. Investors are often surprised to find that tax-deferred plans can outperform taxable investments significantly — if they emphasize no-load mutual funds (with low expense ratios) that are focused on capital appreciation, while keeping bond funds and low-return money-market accounts to a minimum.

Of course, temperament always figures into investment planning. The volatility associated with stocks may steer some people more deeply into the bond camp. This can be acceptable for those who are especially risk-averse (and who have more in the way of overall assets to sustain them). But generally speaking, throughout the course of your investing life, if your emotions don't crumble in the absence of total certainty, the historically higher returns of equity investments[10] argue for a diversified portfolio with a heavy weighting of stocks.

That's especially so if you're young with a steady income and a long time horizon ahead of you before retirement. I'd advise such investors to put as much as they can into stocks, especially right now. With share prices still attractively priced in the current recession, the potential for stocks to outperform bonds substantially is perhaps the most promising since the 1930s. Young investors with courage and the personal discipline to keep investing consistently could wind up breathtakingly wealthy by retirement.

Still, there's no denying the volatility of equity investments — stocks go up; stocks go down — recent events have demonstrated that all too clearly. Stock indices were off as much as 50 percent during 2008, illustrating what investment professionals refer to as the *wider distribution of returns* for stocks (which has to be one of the loveliest euphemisms in all of business). That needn't frighten young investors, though. The long-term trend is always up, and they have time on their

10 The average return on stocks since 1926 has been 10 percent, according to Ibbotson Associates.

side. Asset allocations can be adjusted as they get older and circum-stances change.

A Word About Bonds

While stocks represent corporate ownership — and so generally move in proximate tandem with the fortunes of the companies issuing them (though not necessarily in perfect synchronization) — bonds represent *debt*. When you buy the bonds of a company, institution, government or public agency (such as a school district or municipal authority), you're lending money to that entity, which then takes on a contractual obligation to pay you a particular rate of interest over a specified period and then return your principal at maturity.

Say you buy a 10-year corporate bond. The company will make interest payments every six months until the bond matures, at which time it will return your principal. This is a fixed-income obligation from which the company derives leverage. That is to say, it uses your money to accomplish its business objectives, generating profits in which its owners (the stockholders) will share. Even though the bond gives you no ownership in the company, as a creditor you benefit by preserving your principal while receiving interest on the loan. (Bonds also provide a senior claim on the assets of a corporation in the event of bankruptcy, though that's not a primary consideration as long as you stick with high-quality corporate bonds.)

All of that is simple enough. Things get less clear because bonds aren't always held to maturity, but are bought and sold as investment instruments in the bond market. The main thing to remember about bonds is that the price moves inversely with interest rates. If rates go up, bond prices go down, and vice-versa. Also, the longer the time to maturity, the more volatile is the price of the bond. The price of a 30-year bond will swing quite markedly in response to changes in long-term interest rates, while a 30-day T-Bill won't fluctuate much in price at all.

The great advantage of bonds is "blessed assurance." A bond held to maturity will pay you exactly what you were expecting when you bought it. The only exception is the unlikely event of a default by the issuer — unlikely, though not impossible; some 4 to 5 percent of so-called junk bonds have defaulted historically.[11] AAA-rated corporate bonds, on the other hand, almost never default, and in the case of U.S. Treasury instruments, default isn't a concern at all. The federal government can always cover its obligations through its unique power to print money (even if it generates inflation).

The price of assurance, however, is sacrifice of opportunity. There's no chance that the interest rate on a bond you're holding will go up, and the cost of opportunity missed can be substantial when rates are rising and you're locked in. That cost also increases with time. Say you're holding a 30-year, $1,000 Treasury bond with a 3-percent coupon (the rate of all payments on the bond until its maturity). You can be certain you'll get your 3 percent. But if, during those 30 years, the interest rate on 30-year Treasuries rises to 6 percent (a situation not unthinkable over the course of three decades), the price of your bond will have dropped to $.58 on the dollar.[12]

Still, if your aim is to minimize risk, particularly when you've reached retirement, investing in high-grade bonds is prudent and can help you avoid sleepless nights. Which is why they're an important consideration when it comes to allocating assets. But in the portfolios of most investors with a decent time horizon, the appropriate role for bonds to play is most definitely supportive. You just can't beat stocks for making money.

Your goal in investing should be to increase your assets over time while avoiding being wiped out in any given year. And this is what the

---

11 We never include junk bonds in the portfolios my firm manages, though there are investment advisors who maintain that the higher return potential (as high as stocks, in some cases) justifies the default risk. I prefer it when bonds behave like bonds and don't try to do double duty. I think current conditions justify my approach. Some economists have predicted that 15 percent of junk bonds may default before the current recession has run its course.

12 You don't get "whacked" quite as badly on shorter-maturity bonds. Consider 10-year Treasuries offered at 3.5 percent today. Even if the rate on such bonds doubles (which is quite possible), your principal will only have been devalued to $.83 on the dollar, a much less distressing loss.

right mix of stocks and bonds can accomplish. Stocks provide the appreciation to give you a higher return than bonds over time. But high-grade bonds provide stability of principal and steady income.

A Word About Annuities

One of the most widely marketed financial devices available today is the annuity. Offered by commissioned agents, brokers, insurance representatives, CLUs, registered reps, financial planners, financial advisors, and a wide variety of non-profit organizations involved in education, charity work and even religion, annuities figure prominently in the financial plans of retired folks and those approaching retirement age.

The simple fixed-annuity concept makes sense, and it's very appealing. It's a plan that offers a guaranteed income, generally for the balance of the purchaser's life, in return for a certain amount of money paid up front. Essentially, it's a bet that you're going to outlive your life expectancy as established by the actuarial tables. If your life expectancy is 10 years, and instead you live 20, then you win. If you only make it to five years of that 10-year projection, you lose; your heirs get nothing. Still, assuming that the insurance company that writes and maintains the annuity continues to exist and has the claims-paying ability to make good on its obligation to honor the annuity contract, your income is assured.

The problem with annuities isn't the concept, it's the implementation. Annuities are sold — and sold aggressively. People have come to think of annuities as crucial elements in their retirement strategies for either of two reasons: (1) they have been influenced by the pervasive advertising for various annuity plans; or (2) they have been steered into buying annuities by salesmen working on commission. Those commissions are usually substantial. I've seen them as high as 7 percent of the total amount "invested." And besides the front-end load, there's typically an annual annuity charge, in addition to other fees and expenses that come out of your account. Back-end surrender charges are also common, so if you decide to cash in your annuity, you pay an additional fee just to get your money back. And in all likelihood, what you get back won't be as much as you put in.

Annuities can be fixed or variable. Variable annuities typically have an equity component, which gives you some upside, in that the money is invested in the stock market on your behalf. And in the last few years, a new kind of annuity has appeared, guaranteeing that all your money will be returned at the end of 10 years. That may seem like an extra measure of security, but it's really not such a hot deal. Assuming inflation were to run at a 5-percent annual rate during that 10-year period, the purchasing power of the money returned to you would have been reduced to about $.60 on the dollar. That means $100,000 held for a decade (with no interest) would be equivalent to only about $60,000 — a poor guaranty by any measure.

I have never understood why people choose to give their money to an insurance company; let the company make a profit by investing it; pay commissions, fees, expenses and other charges; and get back only a portion of what they put in originally — and then call this an "investment" account. I think (and I tell my clients) that insurance companies should be used only for actual insurance. Don't pay for an annuity or for any other sort of gimmicky investment-like plan. Instead, buy term insurance — something with low annual premiums that provides coverage against an early death and makes a lump-sum payment. Any extra money should be invested in stock and bond no-load mutual funds. A properly diversified portfolio will vastly outperform the returns provided by an insurance company on any of their so-called "investment products."

chapter 9

Fighting to Win

On December 18, 2008, the editorial board of *The New York Times* took it in mind to mobilize the vast resources of America's "newspaper of record" for a gratuitous swipe at — of all things — the Ave Maria Mutual Funds. The "Old Grey Lady" chided us for our narrow, "unmistakably conservative Catholic outlook," specifically our focus on abortion. The piece drew particular attention to the presence of Tom Monaghan and Phyllis Schlafly on our Catholic Advisory Board — both of whom, of course, are prominent pro-life conservatives.

The language of the editorial is quite revealing of a mindset that has taken hold in the world of contemporary journalism (as in so many other centers of elite opinion), to wit...

> "Ave Maria, whose logo is a cross and open book within a Gothic window, conveys the implicit certainty that its vision of Catholic teaching is the correct one, that it has not misstepped in treading between God and Mammon. But anyone familiar with church politics will see that it stands starkly on one side of the old, deep ideological fault line that divides the church's conservative and liberal wings."
>
> "To oversimplify, one side focuses its moral energies on abortion, contraception and other issues of sexual morality.

The other is more likely also to weigh in on issues like poverty, war, nonviolence and social justice, topics on which Jesus Christ's scriptural record is more explicit."[1]

As if Jesus, having dissuaded the angry crowd from stoning the "woman taken in adultery," decided it really wasn't necessary to tell her she should "go and *sin* no more." What did the Lord care about her sexual choices? Why be so judgmental? It's a theory of Christ's moral priorities which is heard frequently but really doesn't wash.

The editorialists even evoked the memory of Pope John Paul II to cast doubt on our investing philosophy. They suggested that the late Holy Father, as someone who "bestrode these conflicts with stalwart consistency," would certainly have taken a broader view. This was interesting (if dubious) praise from a newspaper that never hesitated to spotlight the relentless criticism which John Paul received during his papacy.

The essay noted that if you scan Ave Maria's investor materials, "you will not find companies like Playboy Enterprises or firms that donate to Planned Parenthood or bestow health benefits on same-sex couples." Then the writers added snidely:

"But you will find United Technologies, which makes Blackhawk helicopters; General Dynamics, builder of Abrams battle tanks and the Stryker combat vehicle; the junk-food giant ConAgra; Exxon Mobil; Halliburton; and Smith & Wesson, one of the largest weapons manufacturers in the world. (Here is a helpful Q. from Smith & Wesson's 'Investor FAQ' Web page: "Does Smith & Wesson still make the 44 Magnum used in the 'Dirty Harry' films? Yes, that gun is the Model 29.)"

---

1   The Board, by the Editorial Writers of *The New York Times*, for Thursday, December 18, 2008 (http://theboard.blogs.nytimes.com).

Unintended Consequences

The piece didn't have quite the effect the keepers of "all the news that's fit to print" might have intended. It generated numerous inquiries about the Ave Maria Mutual Funds, and spurred several other commentators to come to our defense. William Donohue, president of the Catholic League for Religious and Civil Rights,[2] called the editorial "a conservative Catholic-bashing screed," and suggested that its depiction of the Ave Maria logo reflected "an animus against religion." Donohue perceived a certain irony in the *Times* attacking investment vehicles focused on religious ethics "when the American people are being routinely fleeced by unethical investors."

Tom Blumer, a financial-affairs blogger and president of Monetary Matters, an Ohio-based firm that presents workshops on money management, found humor in the list of companies the *Times* chose to note were included or excluded by our screening process. Writing on the conservative website, NewsBusters, he observed, "Apparently, Catholics shouldn't invest in companies involved with a nation's right to self-defense, a person's right to self-defense, or (I guess, re ConAgra) junk food. Who knew?"[3]

But Jeff Benjamin of *Investment News* cut closest to the bone with some simple comparisons of performance in the down market. "The $86 million Ave Maria Growth Fund (AVEGX) has declined by 35.7 percent this year through Monday," he wrote. "This compares to a 36.2 percent decline by the Dow Jones Industrial Average and a 61.9 percent decline by The New York Times Co. stock over the same period." His piece closed with a telling statement: "A call to *The New York Times* was not immediately returned."[4]

---

2   The Catholic League counters media attacks on the Church, Catholic teaching, and Christian beliefs. Donohue's comments are archived online at: http://www.catholicleague.org/ release.php?id=1535.

3   NewsBusters, for Wednesday, December 31, 2008. Blumer's commentary is archived online at: http://newsbusters.org/blogs/tom-blumer/2008/12/31/strikeback-investment-newss-covearge-nyt-blog-post-criticizing-ave-maria. His writings on a variety of subjects can be found on his weblog: http://www.bizzyblog.com.

4   *Investment News*, Tuesday, December 24, 2008. Benjamin's article is archived online at: http://www.investmentnews.com/apps/pbcs.dll/article?AID=/20081224/REG/812249946.

Far be it from me to kick the *Times* when it's down — the stock selling at around $5.00 a share, when last I checked. To be fair, the precipitous decline from $53 a few years back can't be blamed entirely on the hemorrhage of disillusioned readers alienated by the unceasing liberal bias that's as blatant in the *Times'* news columns as in its editorials. It largely reflects the sorry state of mainstream media in general. But then, the New York Times Co. doesn't make the cut in our screening process, anyway. Besides, I've always been a *Wall Street Journal* fan, having read every issue of the last 42 years.

It's hard to single out *The New York Times* for moral confusion when even some people within the Church have trouble arranging their principles in an appropriate order of priority. Writing in the *Catholic Herald,* the newspaper of the Archdiocese of Milwaukee, one Sr. Arlene Welding stated rather shockingly:

> "Obama may be pro-choice, but so is God. God gave everyone a free will, and he does not pressure people into using that free will to do what is right...."
>
> "Yes, abortion is the killing of an innocent life. So is war and violent killing on the street. I have often seen many starving babies in hospitals in Honduras and witnessed their pain. In these cases, abortion might have been the lesser of two evils, and even the most merciful alternative."[5]

I can barely imagine a nun (a member of the School Sisters of St. Francis) being so incapable of discerning the difference between compassion and murder. One might take pity on the poor — indeed, we have a Christian obligation to do so — but life comes before charity. Life comes before everything.

Of course, Sr. Arlene is only one of a veritable legion of Catholics for whom *confusion* would be the kindest word one can attach to their moral perspective. For instance, on the weblog of the *National Catholic Reporter,* writer Kate Childs Graham echoed the spirit, if not

---

5   *Catholic Herald,* Archdiocese of Milwaukee, November 27, 2008 (Vol. 139, No. 41).

the exact words, of Sr. Arlene, observing that she is a pro-choice Catholic "because my Catholic faith tells me I can be." Citing both the *Catechism of the Catholic Church* and St. Thomas Aquinas on the Church's respect for freedom of conscience, she observed, "After years of research, discernment and prayer, my conscience has been well informed. Being a pro-choice Catholic does not contradict my faith; rather, in following my well-informed conscience, I am adhering to the central tenet of Catholic teaching — the primacy of conscience."[6]

So perhaps it would be naive to expect less obtuseness from our news media. Still, it is curious that we should rub *The New York Times* editorial board the wrong way just at the time when we were concentrating our metro New York advertising on the "Laura Ingraham Show." Could there be a connection with the fact that this scrappy young woman is one of the stalwarts of conservative talk radio, the very media segment that's been kicking the stuffings out of *The New York Times* and other print heavyweights?[7]

The question becomes even more intriguing when you consider that the Ave Maria Mutual Funds had been included in a very straightforward report on religiously based investing which ran in *The New York Times* in April 2007. That piece made note of our pro-life orientation, as well as the 7.6-percent return which the Catholic Values Fund had enjoyed over the previous 12 month — with no commentary at all.[8]

But the *Times* editorial writers are hardly the first media voices to question tempering investment decisions with moral concern, Catholic or otherwise. Applying ethical screens to stock analysis has long come under the skeptical gaze of financial writers. For instance,

6   "I am a prochoice Catholic," by Kate Childs Graham, NCROnline, February 26, 2009 (archived at: http://ncronline.org/blogs/young-voices/i-am-prochoice-catholic).

7   Articulate and determined, Laura Ingraham hosts the number-eight-rated radio program on the air. A University of Virginia-trained attorney and former Reagan Administration speechwriter, she strikes me as a younger version of the indefatigable Phyllis Schlafly. The "Laura Ingraham Show" is distributed by Talk Radio Network, which also distributes Michael Savage's "Savage Nation," the number-five-rated program.

8   "Religious Principles Take Root in Funds," *The New York Times*, Sunday, April 8, 2007.

Timothy Middleman, a New York business reporter and radio commentator, offered a succinct rejection of the whole concept. Writing on the financial website, MSN Money Central, nearly three years before the *Times'* rant, Middleman opined, "The idea that screening companies based on non-economic criteria can actually benefit performance — the central claim of socially responsible investing — is baloney."[9]

So, there.

In this book, I have tried to refute the negative assertions, and to explain in detail both the Ave Maria Mutual Funds and my own personal involvement in Morally Responsible Investing. My objectives include attaining good investment results for my Fund shareholders, besides doing some spiritual and moral good. To put it another way, I'm in the game to win. And this has entailed its own set of challenges.

The Investors Speak

In early Fall of 2008, when the smoke signals of market distress were still relatively modest puffs on the horizon, we decided to conduct a survey of our shareholders to determine which stock-screening criteria they considered most important, relative to their own personal moral agendas. Anticipating the need for further diversity in our fund offerings, we had begun looking into overseas investments. Initial research suggested that it would be difficult (if not impossible) for us to apply MRI constraints to stock screening offshore in the way we had been doing it within the United States.

The problem is that corporations based in the European Union and other regions are saddled with government mandates and civic demands that don't permit them the latitude which U.S. companies enjoy in setting their own internal policies. They operate within a profoundly different social and political milieu, which means, for instance, being required by law to extend benefit coverage to non-married partners of employees — heterosexual or homosexual — a cultur-

9 "Your Beliefs and Your Dollars Don't Mix," by Timothy Middleman, MSN Money Central, for Tuesday, February 21, 2006 (archived at: http://b01.moneycentral.msn.com/content/P143801.asp).

al condition which the conservative Catholic journal, *New Oxford Review*, has wryly termed "codified degeneracy."[10] It became clear to us that we would be unfair to tag companies as violators for actions in which they have no choice.

There were further ethical implications, however, which were somewhat more complex. We faced a basic question: Did fidelity to MRI principles require us to forego overseas investing in order to avoid moral taint, or could some adjustment be made which would allow us to provide our shareholders with additional geographic diversity to enhance their investment returns and financial security? This question was a bit of a conundrum, since it touched on stewardship and could be argued on the basis of both moral consistency and fiduciary responsibility.

We knew there was considerable shareholder interest in overseas investment opportunities. But we decided we needed a better sounding on the consciences of our investors before we could proceed to explore how a global fund might be established on a solid moral footing. What concerns did our shareholders — the people whose interests we were striving to serve — think were most important?

In September 2008 we mailed questionnaires to some 7,500 of our shareholders. This was a much larger sampling than was needed to provide a statistically valid profile of our entire investor group, but we wanted to be thorough. As it happens, we found that we had tapped into a deep well of concern. More than 40 percent of survey recipients completed and returned the questionnaires — an uncommonly high level of participation, as surveys go.

I think that this impressive response was triggered by what had happened in the country by the time our questionnaires began arriv-

10 In an article titled "The Vatican Toes the Line," the February 2009 issue of *New Oxford Review* examines a non-binding United Nations declaration introduced by France which aimed at banning all discrimination based on sexual orientation and gender identity and sought universal decriminalization of homosexual acts. Of all nations in Europe, only the Vatican opposed the measure as a veiled first step towards outlawing any criticism of homosexuality, even within the context of Christian moral teaching. Such a move against religious liberty is by no means unprecedented. The article noted how in Canada, a Protestant minister has been legally barred from preaching against homosexuality.

ing at investor mailboxes. The unfolding recession and related discouraging slippage in the markets — resulting from a stunning series of revelations about financial scandals and corporate insolvencies — combined with the anxiety that had been growing throughout the presidential campaign to boost our survey response. Our shareholders were obviously feeling the pressure.

That pressure seems to have influenced the content of their responses, as well. While survey participants recognized the ethical importance of avoiding companies complicit in the weakening of marriage, their paramount concern was about pro-life issues. It was unambiguous — nearly unanimous, in fact. When asked which moral criteria they considered "very important" in screening stocks, 98 percent listed abortion and 96 percent listed contributions to Planned Parenthood. Interestingly, 92 percent listed pornography as well, while only about 50 percent attributed "very important" status to companies providing non-marital partner benefits.

These results were unexpected but — when I thought about it — not really surprising. In a time of heightened economic stress, our shareholders were telling us to pare down to essentials and focus more sharply on the one issue they considered most urgent: *abortion*. Indeed, hundreds of the questionnaires that came back bore handwritten notes reiterating the respondents' concern that their money not be used to support abortion in even the most indirect way.

Facing a Hard Choice

I shared the results of our research with the Catholic Advisory Board at a meeting in November. There ensued a serious and extended discussion of what these investor preferences meant for the Ave Maria Mutual Funds — and not just as related to overseas investments. The message we were receiving from our shareholders went to the very heart of our mission. This constituency was almost exclusively interested in pro-life investing. Opposing abortion and avoiding the corruption of conscience related to it were paramount concerns.

It was striking how much this reflected the vision which Tom Monaghan and Bowie Kuhn had for our first fund back at the beginning. But something else was clear as well: People drawn to Morally Responsible Investing were even more highly motivated to fight the evil of abortion than any of us had assumed.

The essential question we faced was: Had we taken a strict moral stance on an issue which most of our investors viewed as secondary? No doubt, refocusing our moral criteria exclusively on screening out abortion and pornography would make additional stocks available to us — and with the rapidly deteriorating state of the market we were observing in November 2008, that would certainly be an advantage, looking at it purely from an *investing* point of view.

The Board agonized over this quandary, finally arriving at a policy which they felt would allow us to be responsive to our investors' wishes while at least preserving the integrity of our moral intentions. We would screen stocks explicitly on the basis of support for abortion, contributions to organizations promoting abortion, and the production or distribution of pornography. Prohibition of non-marital partner benefits would be retained as a preference. That is to say, if we had to choose between two companies that both had equally good investment characteristics and passed our other moral screens, we would go with the company that didn't offer non-marital partner benefits.

Our mission is the pro-life struggle. It's what our shareholders expect of us, and service to them is both our fiduciary responsibility and our moral obligation. We're focused like a laser on abortion. And the warped arguments put forth by such as Sr. Arlene Welding and Kate Childs Graham (not to mention perverse organizations like the notorious Catholics for a Free Choice) only underscore the necessity of our single-minded approach.

chapter 10

The Bottom Line

Investors' reactions to the Ave Maria Mutual Funds range from very negative to resoundingly positive. Some folks will reject the entire concept of Morally Responsible Investing out of hand. They may recoil from anything that smacks of religion, Catholic or otherwise. They may be thoughtlessly enamored of "a woman's right to choose." Or they may assume that any sort of non-economic screening criteria must necessarily present an insurmountable obstacle to investment success. Whatever their preconceptions, they are unlikely ever to be part of our shareholder community.

At the other end of the spectrum are those who burst with enthusiasm as soon as they hear about our funds. Perhaps they're naturally disposed toward projects with a Catholic (or at least a spiritual) character. Perhaps they're fiercely committed to the pro-life cause — in which case, surprisingly enough, some don't even care all that much about the investment results.

In between those two poles there's a large group of people who could be prospects for our funds, if they were convinced that what we have to offer is valid — that Morally Responsible Investing really is effective in the service of both conscience and investment success. It is these folks I've had in mind while developing this book. After all, most people are interested in making money, whatever their religious affinities. Likewise, most people are moral in their business dealings, so there is something inherently intriguing about the idea of tying investments to a larger moral vision.

I have found this to be especially true in my dealings with institutional investors. The people who manage institutional investments are charged with obtaining good performance, so they must act prudently. It's incumbent upon them to exercise due diligence. They must carefully examine the track record of any fund under consideration, and investigate the people running it. No one with such a fiduciary responsibility is free to choose a mutual fund merely because it's Catholic, not even those managing investments for Catholic organizations.

However, most investment professionals are aware that their financial choices do not exist entirely apart from the missions of the institutions they represent. This has been a significant advantage to us in gaining entry to the inner circles of decision making within some of the nation's most respected foundations and charitable groups. The result is that over 300 institutions, mostly Catholic, have invested anywhere from $10,000 to $20 million in the Ave Maria Mutual Funds. That's a substantial testament of faith in the MRI concept. It's especially significant because it reflects the judgments of people whose professional lives are spent evaluating every conceivable type of opportunity. It hasn't happened by accident. My colleagues and I have had to make our case. We've had to explain our investing process and prove that it works.

Investment Research is Crucial

In contrast to much financial-services marketing these days, our presentation does not depend on propagating any illusions of mystery about what we do. We don't invoke the razzle-dazzle of impressive, technical-sounding jargon. We make no pretensions to special insights, nor do we imply secret access to "inside information." And we do not claim superior skills with which to *time* the market (let me say it again: market timing is mostly a loser's game). Actually, we make it plain that our methods are quite simple and transparent, based mostly on hard work.

An important advantage we *do* have — one that allows us to make investment decisions that are both financially astute and morally appropriate (and the one which most individual investors *don't* have) — is institutional investment research. As a mutual fund management company, Schwartz Investment Counsel, Inc. has the resources to acquire sophisticated research services. We utilize information provided by a variety of leading Wall Street firms and regional boutique brokerage houses in assessing the investment merits of thousands of companies. The data acquired from such sources, added to the work of our own analysts, provides the basis for sound professional judgment in mutual fund management.

Separately, in following the moral guidelines established by our Catholic Advisory Board, we use several commercially available screening services. One of our main sources is Institutional Shareholder Services (ISS), a leading proxy-advisory firm. ISS, which was recently acquired by RiskMetrics Group[1], a provider of risk-management products and services to participants in financial markets around the world, might be thought of as the CIA of Wall Street. These folks are adept at ferreting out all kinds of company data, including intelligence on products and markets, corporate management, credit, accounting, legal issues — though not the investment merits of a particular company at any point in time (our in-house analysts and portfolio managers make those determinations). ISS serves more than 2,300 institutions and 1,000 corporate clients in some 50 countries (from 19 research locations).

The area of their expertise that touches us is an ability to identify what's called ESG (environmental, social and governance) factors. These include corporate policies and practices bearing on such concerns as energy use, political contributions, labor and human rights issues, and other items relevant to mutual funds that have ethical inter-

---

1 Further information about research services provided by RiskMetrics Group can be found online at: http://www.riskmetrics.com.

ests. Most of these "values-based criteria" are the province of the "socially responsible" funds. But among them are faith-based considerations which we have specified as essential to our moral screens. We receive customized research reports that are truly exhaustive in detail. And the scope of information available is astounding. If I wanted to know how a particular company's manufacturing operations impacted the breeding patterns of turtles during the year 1989, I think that data could be obtained.

Without such a comprehensive perspective available to us, it would be virtually impossible to ascertain whether companies have morally objectionable policies and practices. Incidentally, between 10 and 15 percent of companies whose stocks are held by most mutual funds, including the largest and most widely marketed, would not pass Ave Maria's moral screens. Naturally, the costs associated with the various screening services we use are high: tens of thousands of dollars per year. So, as the old safety-warning cliché cautions, "Don't try this at home."

Fund Performance[2]

Combining this depth of corporate intelligence with the security-analysis principles of Value Investing discussed in Chapter Five allows us to identify issues that can be productive additions to our portfolios. In the MRI approach, *value* and *values* really are complementary concepts. When we complete our fundamental security analysis, feel we've identified a company that has good business characteristics (and all the other criteria we're looking for), and determine that the valuation is reasonable, we check to see if the company is an offender before we buy its stock.

The result has been better-than-average performance, even in the face of market disaster. I'm especially proud to note that the Ave Maria Growth Fund received the 2009 Lipper Fund Award as number-one among 653 funds in its category (MultiCap Core) for the three years

2   See Appendix C for a description of Morningstar ratings and for information on the performance of the Ave Maria Mutual Funds through December 31, 2009.

162

ending December 31, 2008.[3] Similarly, the Ave Maria Rising Dividend Fund remains one of the best performing mutual funds in the country. As of Fall 2009, these funds were five-star rated by Morningstar — and that was *after* the stock market debacle of 2008 and early 2009.

Now to be sure, both funds were down in 2008: the Rising Dividend Fund down 22 percent, and the Growth Fund down 32 percent. But then, they both beat the S&P 500, which was down 37 percent. Relatively, our funds were winners. During 2008, the Rising Dividend Fund was in the top 1 percentile of all funds in its category, as ranked by Morningstar (number four out of 352). For the three-year period ended December 31, 2008, it ranked in the top 2 percentile, among 286 mutual funds in its category.

Pointing out that you're hurting less than the other guys is a hard sell. I never thought I'd brag about losing only 22 percent of our shareholders' money in a year. But compare our funds with the state of the overall market, which by early 2009 had seen the Dow cut in half, or even with the performance of mutual funds in general — down 38 percent overall from a year earlier — and we look really good. The Ave Maria Growth Fund ranked 24th among 769 funds in 2008, while it was 21st among 687 funds for the three-year period ended December 31, 2008. And so with each of our equity mutual funds. Investment performance, both short-term and long-term, has been above average. In 2008, each of our equity funds beat its respective benchmark.

To grasp the true power of the MRI concept, we must look back before this period of market turmoil, during which virtually every aspect of the world economy has been so battered. The years since 2001, when the Ave Maria Catholic Values Fund was started, have been eventful. We've experienced: 9/11 and a series of other violent expressions of Islamist extremism around the world; subsequent wars in Afghanistan and Iraq; the rise of leftist dictatorship in Venezuela;

---

3 The Lipper Award, given by Lipper Analytical Services, a subsidiary of the Thomson Reuters global news organization, recognized the Ave Maria Growth Fund for delivering the strongest risk-adjusted performance, calculated with dividends reinvested and without sales charges. As the requisite disclaimer always states, results are historical and do not guarantee future results.

what looks like a neo-Stalinist revival in Russia. In our domestic politics, the country moved from a center-right, Reaganesque populism vital enough to survive the moral depredations of Bill Clinton, to the Democratic Party's government takeover. There was also that collapse in oil prices from $150 to $32 per barrel, and of course, the stock implosion of late 2008 and early 2009.

For all their wild drama, the years prior to the market meltdown are much closer to economic conditions we would recognize as appropriate to the normal functioning of our economy than are what has happened since Fall 2008. So a thorough judgment of Morally Responsible Investing requires a longer view: the entire period since each of the Ave Maria Mutual Funds was launched. And over that time, our funds have outpaced the market, some quite handily.

Since its inception on May 1, 2001, through December 31, 2009, the Ave Maria Catholic Values Fund has produced an annual return of 5.25%, versus 0.44% for the S&P 500. Meanwhile, the Ave Maria Growth Fund has produced an annualized rate of return of 7.98% versus 5.07% for the S&P 500, since its inception on May 1, 2003. And in the five-year period ended December 31, 2009, it had an annual return of 2.16%, versus 0.42% for the S&P 500. This is really quite extraordinary, particularly considering that, for the ten-year period ended December 31, 2009, the S&P 500 Index produced a negative annual return of -0.95%.

Some would argue that this demonstrates that stocks are no longer a good investment. I say just the opposite. The fact that the S&P 500 had ten years of poor performance dramatically increases the likelihood that the next ten years will be considerably better, very likely beating the long-term average return on equities of 10 percent per year. A reversion to the mean would indicate that the next ten years would produce 12–14 percent compound annual returns.

I believe that the future investment performance of the Ave Maria Mutual Funds will continue to be superior to that of the market in general, defying the expectations of those who think that saddling ourselves with moral constraints (screening out abortion and pornography) necessarily limits our investing options or somehow leaves us only bad companies in which to put our shareholders' money. Our performance record speaks for itself.

Professionalism Shows

The good investment-management practices, good fundamental research by our analysts, and good execution of sound investment strategies — all the procedures I have described in this book — must be counted as factors in this enviable performance. But if I had to highlight one single reason we've done as well as we have, I think it would be this: We keep our investment goals and our moral aims in balance. As I have said many times, especially whenever I've been interviewed by the media, my staff and I are not theologians, nor do we hold ourselves out as experts on Church teaching. We are investment professionals, a group of CFAs and MBAs with many years of experience in managing other people's money.[4]

This separation of financial objectives and philosophical commitment is not apparent in most "socially responsible" funds, nor even in other religiously inspired funds with a moral purpose. A conversation I had some years ago with the manager of an Evangelical mutual fund brings this point into focus. The fund had been designed specifically to avoid, among other vices, investments in alcohol-related stocks. And such was the manager's dedication to eradicating "evil rum," as he put it, that financial returns were a distinctly secondary consideration.

"Alcohol has destroyed so many lives and hurt so many people, it's ruining the world," he said. "This is my mission, and I believe in it with all my heart."

He was a truly devoted Christian man, but he was a poor mutual fund manager, and that lack of professionalism was reflected in the poor performance of his fund. I, on the other hand, am intensely con-

---

4 We depend on the guidance of our Catholic Advisory Board, which is composed of prominent lay Catholics, some of whom do have theological credentials, but all of whom are loyal to the Magisterium. So we have plenty of moral fire power when it comes to Catholic theology and doctrine, especially as it relates to pro-life and pro-family matters.

cerned about investment performance. I want to produce the best returns possible for our shareholders, and I believe that's the best way to accomplish our religiously inspired mission and reach our moral goals. We've made noteworthy progress in that direction.

Questions have been raised about applying MRI to direct management of institutional investment portfolios. Some Church organizations that have participated in our funds — particularly some dioceses — have inquired about the possibility of crafting individually tailored investment portfolios to meet their specific investment objectives. I believe this is perfectly practical, since we can readily draw on the systems and procedures already in place for our funds and functioning so well. Consequently, we are in the process of developing what we call Separately Managed Accounts for institutional clients. A Separately Managed Account has a lower expense ratio associated with it, as little as half what we must charge to manage our mutual funds. But it requires a correspondingly higher minimum level of participation — *much* higher: possibly $20 million, as opposed to the $1,000 mutual fund minimum commitment.

Whether Separately Managed Accounts will become a significant part of our practice remains to be seen. But I am confident enough in Morally Responsible Investing to believe it can have many applications. The bottom line is: *It works!*

chapter 11

Conclusion

Given the turmoil that's engulfed our economy, this may seem like an odd time to bring out an investment book. The confidence required to put hard-earned money into the securities of companies so shaken in recent months has surely been tested. And at the time these words are written, it looks like there are more tests ahead. Peter J. Tanous, president of the Washington, DC-based, Lynx Investment Advisory LLC, has written that to recover in five years the losses suffered in just a year and a half (from the market's high of October 2007 to the levels of March 2009) would require sustained annual returns of over 18 percent — and "there are few periods in stock market history when the market rose 18 percent for five years."[1]

And yet, despite witnessing so much money evaporate so quickly, from a Value Investing perspective, this is a uniquely propitious moment. Stock prices have been grossly distorted by factors that do not reflect the actual strength and resilience of American industry.

---

1   "How Long Until Stocks Bounce Back?" by Peter J. Tanous, *The Wall Street Journal*, Monday, March 30, 2009. Tanous' projection is something less than buoyant, but he offers impatient investors a bit of sound advice: "Raising the risk level of your investments to accelerate gains will set you up for even greater losses if your risky investments don't work out. Instead, allocate your assets wisely, and be mindful of the risks in the different asset classes you choose."

There is still an abundance of under-valued companies whose shares are languishing at price levels considerably below their intrinsic value. For investors with courage and patience, bargains are everywhere.

This simple fact remains: For most people, the stock market is the most efficient vehicle for creating wealth ever conceived. Back in 1991, my colleague, Rick Platte, who serves as lead portfolio manager for the five-star-rated Ave Maria Rising Dividend Fund, wrote a market commentary on investment prospects in an economy battered by recession and the first Gulf War; he updated it in 2001, after the "dot-com bust." In it, he noted the swings in investor attitudes, from wild euphoria to abject fear, which had left investors in similar states of shellshock at both points in market history. Rick's observations remain pertinent:

> "The question would seem to be, on which of these two diametrically opposing views of the market [optimism or pessimism] should investors be basing their investment decisions? Neither, in our estimation. Why? Because they both represent a very fickle popular sentiment, and are the product of a very temporary view of the economy and equity market. It is our contention that investors should focus on the long-term perspective, and if they do, they will be drawn to significant ownership of high-quality common stocks."

> "When one takes a short-term view of either the economy or the stock market, it is easy to be alternately immobilized and stampeded by changing market psychology and momentary impressions of the economic environment. The often-overlooked facet of this phenomenon is that the market discounts the consensus view, be it positive or negative. So if investors are, in the aggregate, frightened by prospects for the economy, stock prices move lower to reflect that view. Conversely, when optimism reigns, high stock prices reflect that, too."

> "Taking the longer-term perspective has the effect of smoothing out many of the bumps and eliminating much of

the noise one is subjected to when attempting to make decisions based upon short-term views. There is risk in stocks. They go up, and they go down. But, over the long term, the financial significance of recessions and even wars is vastly diminished, as the predominant trend for stock prices is up."[2]

Rick provided a small chart that demonstrated the comparative returns on $1.00 invested in various asset classes, showing what each investment would have been worth relative to the average rate of inflation since 1926. The figures are quite striking.

Here the comparisons are extended to the end of 2008:

Comparative Investment Returns[3]

	$1.00 INVESTED IN 1926	MARKET VALUE IN 1989	MARKET VALUE IN 2008	COMPOUND ANNUAL RETURN 1926-2008
Common Stocks	$1.00	$534	$2,049	9.6%
Long-term Treasury Bonds	$1.00	$17	$99	5.7%
Treasury Bills	$1.00	$9	$21	3.7%
Rate of Inflation	$1.00	$7	$12	3.0%

The chart makes it abundantly clear: Even allowing for the 2008 market debacle and every other recession that has occurred in more than eight decades of market tracking (including the crash of 1929), equities are far and away the most productive type of investment over time. And that holds true whether you invest in individual stocks or mutual funds. Research by Ann Arbor, Michigan-based Exchange Capital Management (conducted over a somewhat shorter time span) mirrors this upward trend. Analyzing stock market performance in comparison with interest rates and 10-year Treasury yields during peri-

---

2   "A Case for Common Stocks" by Richard J. Platte, Jr., CFA. Rick's commentary was distributed to clients of Schwartz Investment Counsel, Inc. as part of our ongoing investor-communications effort. It is reproduced in full as an appendix to this book.

3   Source: Ibbotson Associates, a subsidiary of Morningstar.

ods of both growth and recession between 1964 and 2006, ECM found, "From a peak-to-peak or trough-to-trough basis, stock prices reliably trend close to 6½ percent per year.... That price appreciation plus the dividend yield gets you to the long-run total return of the stock market of 10 percent."[4]

Jeremy Siegel, from the University of Pennsylvania's Wharton School, makes the same point in his best selling investment book, *Stocks for the Long Run*:

> "The long-term perspective radically changes one's view of the risk of stocks. The short-term fluctuations in the stock market, which loom so large to investors when they occur, are insignificant when compared to the upward movement of equity values over time."[5]

Investment advisor Steven Selengut of the South Carolina-based Sanco Services, Inc., goes a step further. Writing for the online journal TCS Daily, he notes: "There has never been a correction that has not proven to be an investment opportunity." Selengut and I would differ somewhat in our approaches to market analysis, but I admire the clarity with which he perceives both current conditions and the human reality that guarantees a market rebound...

> "We'll be using credit cards, driving cars and motorcycles, drinking beer, and buying clothes 20 years from now. Very few interest payments have been missed and surprisingly few divi-

---

4   "The Road from Perdition" by Michael R, Reid, Kevin D. McVeigh, and Anthony J. DiGiovanni (January 2009); Exchange Capital Management, Inc, Ann Arbor, Michigan. In case 2008-09 has you anticipating a return of 1930s market conditions, the ECM advisory points out that we've already seen that scenario repeated, twice in fact. "The cyclical trough of the stock market in the Great Depression was matched in the '70s and again in the '80s," the authors write, "while the recent plunge in stocks has taken us very close to hitting the bottom end of the range yet again." In other words, we've survived it all before, and will do so again.

5   *Stocks for the Long Run* by Jeremy J. Siegel, The McGraw Hill Companies, 2007.

dends eliminated. Only the prices have changed, to preserve the long-term reality of things...."[6]

He even declares that market corrections are "beautiful things" — a bold assertion when account statements are looking anything but beautiful. But he's right. At the depths of the 2008-09 downturn, when capital had fled the markets in a massive liquidation of equities worse than anything I'd ever seen in four decades of investment counsel, the inevitability of recovery was apparent. Some $4 trillion of investor cash was sitting in money market funds as shelter against further loss, the highest cash-to-equity market value on record. You might think that's a sign of utter doom: 40 percent of market capitalization cringing in fear of total destruction to come. But it's really the portent of a future bull market. Such a mountain of liquidity cannot sit squirreled away indefinitely, because money can't be idle forever. Investors will ultimately seek opportunities to make their cash productive, and that need will always take them back to the stock market.

In fact, as Jim Margard, chief investment officer for the Seattle-based, Rainier Investment Management, Inc., has put it, "The big risk today is *not* owning stock." Interviewed by *The Wall Street Journal,* Margard observed that too many people invest "with their eye on the rearview mirror, rather than anticipating the direction the economy will be taking two or three quarters into the future."[7]

Even if there are more bumps and slides ahead, in the words of my colleague, Rick Platte," the predominant trend for stock prices is up." Recovery *will* come.

---

6   "Stock Market Corrections are Beautiful— and Necessary" by Steven Selengut, TCS Daily, for April 16, 2009 (available online at: http://www.tcsdaily.com/article.aspx ?id=041609A). Selengut is the author of *The Brainwashing of the American Investor,* W&A Publishing (2007).

7   "Why Investing Still Makes Sense," by Randy Myers, *The Wall Street Journal,* Friday, April 3, 2009.

The Upside of the Downturn

While market performance and investment potential are critical considerations, the particular focus of this book is *faith*. In these pages I have addressed the desire to pursue capital market gains in a way that does not compromise conscience. Moreover, I've called for a great movement of investors who are motivated by religious commitment to act in concert, exerting pressure on the business community for the sake of positive moral change. And this may be the best of all times to be promoting such a movement.

Both history and our parents have told us that during the Great Depression of the 1930s, families grew closer. Sometimes they became *literally* closer, with multiple generations moving in together and sharing living expenses when someone lost a home. More often they provided assistance, stretching resources that had become tight. The current recession has already promoted this kind of inter-generational sharing. And if economic stress persists for a long time, we will very likely see a resurgence of the extended family.

Living with the folks undoubtedly produces stress (think mother-in-law and daughter-in-law under one roof), but it also conduces toward greater communication. Almost in spite of themselves, people open up to each other about their ideas, hopes and dreams. They reveal their values, even if they sometimes reveal them at high volume. Also, living with Grandma and Grandpa gives children the benefit of a longer time perspective as they learn the family story and gain an understanding of their roots — especially their religious roots.

I'm no sociologist, but my gut tells me that this sort of togetherness has to encourage the transmission of faith. Even if Mom and Dad fell away from the Church and the kids were never baptized, Granny getting up every morning for daily Mass provides an ongoing witness to the importance of religion. This can have profound effects over time: on the spirituality of the household, on the level of moral behavior among family members, and ultimately on the faith decisions the kids will make for themselves.

Catholic Advisory Board member, Phyllis Schlafly — the strongest pro-family advocate I know — has written and spoken extensively about family breakdown, which she notes is intimately connected with a general decline of spirituality throughout our culture and a disheartening breakdown in moral standards and civil behavior. Phyllis points to the collapse of discipline in schools, rising crime rates, increases in poverty, all of which correlate with the destruction of families. If this recession has the effect of strengthening family life, we could find ourselves counting it as a great and unexpected blessing. And wouldn't *that* be ironic?

For my part, I think a restoration of "family values" (that most overworked of clichés, but nonetheless a phrase that captures a real and persistent human longing) would be a tremendous encouragement both to the pro-life movement and to Morally Responsible Investing. Investors — Catholics and Protestants alike — may well be more inclined to add a moral component to their portfolios. Under such conditions, the effort I seek to mount in defense of life becomes ever more plausible. In a turn on one of the more cynical sound bites to emerge during the early days of the Obama regime, it would be a matter of not letting a good crisis go to waste.

The business community *can* be influenced, because it is responsive to a force other than politics — that is, to *money*. Certainly, corporations have been buffeted by any number of ideological fads. Those of us who lived through the great era of "sensitivity training" can attest to the impact of politics on business. And it's clear enough that most of the current emphasis on the "greening" of corporations is not only irrelevant to the actual concerns of businesses, it actually runs counter to plain economic sense.

For all of that, the ongoing requirement of profit makes companies much less willing to jump through the flaming hoops of intellectual whim than, say, public agencies or academic institutions. It also makes them more responsive to the native practicality of those ordinary folks from whom their profits (and capital) come. Tom Monaghan and Bowie Kuhn were entirely right when they insisted, back at the start of the Ave Maria Mutual Funds, that a group of like-minded, motivated investors can make a difference, acting together with dedication and perseverance. And as our popes and serious Catholic scholars such as

George Weigel, Robert George and Michael Novak have demonstrated, a climate of moral consistency and uplift is as important to business success as it is to the wellbeing of society in general.

Over the better part of a decade, we have demonstrated that an investment program operated within constraints determined by the concept of Morally Responsible Investing can show an excellent return. Our funds have performed well in up-markets, and suffered less in the disastrous market downturn of 2008-2009. In explanation of this reassuring performance I can only offer my belief that there is a relationship between ethics and business results. Over time, those companies that are well managed tend to be the most successful, and morality is a vital component of good management.

This view is not completely impervious to quibbling, but it has a pedigree reaching all the way back through Adam Smith (who linked such moral virtues as prudence, justice, industry, frugality and constancy with the satisfaction of self-interest), through the rabbinic sages (who waxed poetic on commercial ethics in page after page of the Talmud), to the Golden Rule and its firm foundation, the Ten Commandments. Indeed, the truth of my assertion has only been underscored by the all-too-numerous moral lapses that helped bring the country to its current state of economic distress.

The Holy Father himself has weighed in strongly on this point. In his paper delivered to that 1985 symposium in Rome, then-Cardinal Ratzinger stated unequivocally that "market rules function only when a moral consensus exists and sustains them." He observed that a long and woeful secularist tradition has fostered the specious idea that, even if they have faith, people in business should "regard their Christianity as a private concern, while as members of the business community they abide by the laws of the economy." He rejected this false dichotomy, declaring prophetically:

"It is becoming an increasingly obvious fact of economic history that the development of economic systems which concentrate on the common good depends on a determinate ethical system, which in turn can be born and sustained only by strong religious convictions. Conversely, it has also become obvious that the decline of such discipline can actually cause the laws of the market to collapse. An economic policy that is ordered not only to the good of the group — indeed, not only to the common good of a determinate state — but to the common good of the family of man demands a maximum of ethical discipline and thus a maximum of religious strength."[8]

Business *does* have a dog in the morality fight, because business stands on culture, and the basis of culture is religion ("cult"). As David P. Goldman, the *Asia Times'* commentator who styles himself "Spengler," has noted, those cultures in which people exhibit the optimism made possible by spiritual confidence — America foremost among them — are still experiencing both population growth and economic expansion, even if they are somewhat slowed by the current recession. It is Christianity, with its insistence on the transformative power of faith and individual moral responsibility, that makes such confidence possible. Those cultures that have lost spiritual vitality through the decline of faith, or where religion binds people to tribal patterns and social norms that deny the inherent dignity of individual life, stand on the brink of economic collapse.[9]

Religiously motivated investors thus have a strong case to make, and we must not shrink from making it. While it might take organized effort to accomplish our goal, the moral cause in which we seek to enlist American business is clearly for business' benefit.

---

8   The pope's paper, "Market Economy and Ethics" by Joseph Cardinal Ratzinger (1985), was originally published in English by *Communio* (Fall 1986). It is available online from The Acton Institute (http://www.acton.org/publications/occasionalpapers/publicat_occasionalpapers_ratzinger.php?view=print).

9   "Overcoming Ethnicity" by David P. Goldman, *Asia Times*, Monday, January 6, 2009, archived online at the Asia Times website (http://www.atimes.com/atimes/Front_Page/KA06Aa01.html). Goldman, associate editor for the Catholic journal, *First Things* (who until recently contributed to *Asia Times* under the pseudonym, "Spengler," after the *early* 20th-Century German historian and philosopher, Oswald Spengler), notes that the economic, political and social dynamism of China and India, two countries that share the multi-ethnic character of the United States, are thriving in large measure because of the growing influence of Christianity among their peoples.

Getting Good Returns

This is our moment. The stressed condition of the economy has given investors of conscience a chance not only to avoid stocks tainted by moral ambiguity, but also to become a significant presence on the American financial scene through strategic joint action. And not just Catholics, by any means. Despite the distinctively Catholic name, the Ave Maria Mutual Funds have never been sectarian. We have always sought to reach across denominational lines, and the opportunity currently before us provides encouragement to redouble our efforts to attract non-Catholic investors.[10]

In this way we can help to reinforce the interfaith unity of the pro-life movement which has suffered some noticeable erosion. Differences in belief are important, to be sure, and cannot be papered over. But what could be better than mutual economic interest to cement relationships between people who share faith and a set of values so much more fundamental than the points of doctrine on which they differ? Our common commitment, after all, is to God and to His most precious gift: life. Morally Responsible Investing is a tool with which we can serve Him together and see to the protection of that gift.

It's already happening. I estimate that about ten percent of our 25,000 shareholders are non-Catholics, and we receive inquiries from more such folks all the time — though there is often an air of hesitancy about those contacts. I remember getting a call from a Protestant minister in the early days of the Ave Maria Catholic Values Fund. He asked me very sheepishly, "Do you have to be Catholic to invest in your fund?"

"Of course not," I replied. "We don't discriminate against anybody."

"Oh, thank God," he said. "One of my clergy colleagues and I want to invest in your fund because we're strongly pro-life. The Catholic Values Fund is the only Mutual Fund I know of that has such

---

10 I should note that the Schwartz Investment Counsel, Inc. staff includes individuals of various Christian denominations. For instance, Rick Platte, who has worked with me since 1979, is Presbyterian and an Elder in his church.

a strong pro-life stance. Send us a prospectus and application. We'll put a check in the mail to you immediately."

While abortion was a marginal issue in the last election, polls tell us that there was a significant percentage of voters who saw it as a key concern, specifically those people who attend church regularly, are active in their faith communities, and hold traditional moral views. That's our constituency. I'm convinced the investors are out there, enough to build a movement that can eventually achieve a critical mass.

This is no quixotic crusade, and I am no pie-in-the-sky idealist. I don't propose to lead morally flaccid corporate managers back to the path of rectitude with promises of large stock purchases. Nor do I wish to find weak companies and somehow build them into moral and economic powerhouses. I've been in the investment-counseling profession too long to indulge those kinds of fantasies. What I know we *can* do is identify companies that have both good investment merits and policies that are consistent with MRI principles, and then support them with our investment capital. In this way we will become an important shareholder bloc whose contentment corporate managers will recognize is in their best interest to ensure.

Influencing corporate behavior is not easy, but neither is it impossible. Anti-abortion activist, Tom Strobhar, president of the Dayton, Ohio-based investment firm, Pro-Vita Advisors (another source from which we draw company information for our moral screening process), has succeeded in persuading several major companies to stop donating to Planned Parenthood. One of his biggest hits was American Express. And I was present when Strobhar confronted Warren Buffett, taking the microphone at a Berkshire Hathaway annual meeting to chastise the great man for his abortion support — in front of 22,000 shareholders. Such effort and the boldness behind it are to be admired greatly.

I myself have had many conversations with corporate managers about the moral implications of their companies' policies and practices. And while I have indeed encountered executives who simply don't care (or in some cases are actively opposed to the points of principle I raise), more than once I have seen my words elicit genuine surprise. Unlikely as it might seem in sophisticated business leaders, the negative societal effects of what their companies do sometimes just haven't occurred to them, because they are accustomed to thinking in the dualistic way noted by then-Cardinal Ratzinger: issues of business belong here; moral truths belong there.

Our job is to make such essentially good-hearted people see the connections. As for those who are more willfully resistant, there are other kinds of pressures which can eventually be brought to bear — recall the stockholder action against South African apartheid.

In any event, we can gain influence by being practical investors. And as we increase in numbers and extend our influence to more and more companies, we will — like the mustard seed that, in the parable, grew to enormous size — achieve greater presence and stronger impact over an ever wider area. It is within our capability to have a positive effect on society, because we can touch business in a positive way. And we can have a positive effect on business because Morally Responsible Investing works. It works by combining the desire for economic security with moral volition to reach a Christian end.

Things change — and nothing more surprisingly or more dramatically than economic conditions. I believe now is the time to get into the market in a big way, to commit resources to equities that have significant price-appreciation potential.

Capitalism is the only economic system that works. In truth it's the only economic system there is, because it's the only one that reflects the real actions of real people. All other systems ever proposed (Communism, especially) are abstract theories based on supposition, conjecture and good wishes detached from human reality. Only markets reflect what people actually do to advance their own financial interests. Investors disheartened by economic downturns will be amazed to witness the excellent performance of fine companies as the capital markets continue their long term upward trend, periodic and normal setbacks notwithstanding.

If we act now, with purpose and with prudence, we can make investment returns that are truly good — in the financial sense and in a much larger ethical sense, as well. To adapt another famous parable, what I propose for Christian investors — and what I believe we can accomplish — is to build a great economic house on the rock of faith, of commitment, of sound and proven investment practices, and in so doing, to extend a great moral influence throughout the business community.

Jesus told us that we have the ability to read the signs of the times. And as Christians we are called upon to act. Those of us who have the means to do so *must* act...

> "The servant who knows his master's will and does not get ready or does not do what his master wants will be beaten with many blows.... From everyone who has been given much, much will be demanded; and from the one who has been entrusted with much, more will be asked." (Luke 12:47-48)

A Case for Common Stocks (1991)

By Richard L. Platte, Jr. CFA

A month ago, most investors were hesitant to invest in common stocks. With war in the Middle East, the economy in recession, a worsening S&L crisis and consumer confidence slipping to levels not seen since the 30s, pessimism was everywhere. In the euphoric month since then, the psychology of the market has been dramatically reversed, and there has been a stampede into stocks. Portfolio managers, afraid of being left behind with large cash positions, have chased stocks higher.

Investment fundamentals have changed very little in the intervening month. What has changed is investor perception. The question would seem to be, on which of these two diametrically opposing views of the market should investors be basing their investment decisions.

Neither, in our estimation. Why? Because they both represent a very fickle popular sentiment, and are the product of a very temporary view of the economy and equity market. It is our contention that investors should focus on the long-term perspective, and if they do, they will be drawn to significant ownership of high-quality common stocks.

When one takes a short-term view of either the economy, or the stock market, it is easy to be alternately immobilized and stampeded by changing market psychology, and momentary impressions of the economic environment. The often overlooked facet of this phenomenon is that the market discounts the consensus view, be it positive or negative. So, if the investors are, in the aggregate, frightened by prospects for the economy, stock prices move lower to reflect that view. Conversely, when optimism reigns, high stock prices reflect that too.

Taking the longer-term perspective has the effect of smoothing out many of the bumps and eliminating much of the noise one is subjected to when attempting to make decisions based upon short-term views. There is risk in stocks. They go up, and they go down. But, over the long term, the financial significance of recessions and even wars, is vastly diminished as the predominant trend for stock prices is up.

The following table, which is from Ibbotson Associates, summarizes the compound annual return for each of the major asset categories, over the period from 1926 - 1989.

Comparative Investment Returns

	$1.00 INVESTED IN 1926	MARKET VALUE IN 1989	COMPOUND ANNUAL RETURN 1926-1989
Common Stocks	$1.00	$534.46	10.3%
Long-term Treasury Bonds	$1.00	$17.30	4.6%
Treasury Bills	$1.00	$9.67	3.6%
Rate of Inflation	$1.00	$7.04	3.1%

Clearly, stocks outperformed other financial assets by a wide margin during a time span which included depressions and wars. Fortunately, it isn't necessary to invest for 64 years in order to achieve favorable results in common stocks. During most five-year periods within this 64 year time span, the return on stocks easily surpassed the return on bonds, cash equivalents and inflation.

Perhaps the greatest risk investors face when investing in common stocks is that they become preoccupied with efforts to make short-term calls on the stocks market and in so doing dilute the positive impact of long-term common stock investing. Those who focus on the long-term, and are financially and psychologically able to absorb the volatility of common stocks, will continue to be richly rewarded.

A Case for Common Stocks (2001)

By Richard L. Platte, Jr. CFA

Ten years ago, we wrote our first commentary entitled "A Case for Common Stocks." It argued for long-term ownership of quality common stocks. Ten years ago, the U.S. economy was emerging from recession and the Gulf War had just concluded. Investors were alternately depressed and euphoric. In that sense, the period was very similar to the present, though the sequence has been reversed. But we got through the doubts; the economy delivered a decade of unprecedented growth, and investors came to expect double-digit annual returns from stocks. Times were good and no one thought much about whether or not to hold equities, the answer was obvious.

Now the economy is flirting with recession, and the direction in equity prices is down. (How long has it been since you've heard anyone suggest buying on the dips?) In this environment, investors are re-examining the wisdom of stock ownership, some are selling, and a few have no regrets.

Given all of the excesses of recent years and the subsequent collapse of the Internet stocks, not to mention the meltdown of the Nasdaq, investors have lost track of the fundamental reason for owning equities long term. In the recent bubble, stock valuations for the popular stocks were rising so rapidly that earnings didn't matter in any specific sense. It didn't really matter exactly what Cisco was going to earn, investors — ah, make that speculators — were eagerly buying it, because it was going up. Everyone was buying Cisco. In the case of the Internet stocks, earnings *really* didn't matter because there were no earnings. "Vision" and notions of the new economy ruled the day. Of such are bubbles made. It had to end and it did.

The excesses of that period are now being unwound. It is in the midst of the resultant carnage that investors are wondering if the case for long-term ownership of common stocks is still valid. If so, is now a good time to buy? The answer in both cases is yes. In recent years, we were advocates of caution, concerned about the decline of discipline and the advance of speculation in the equities market. Nevertheless, during that period, we remained convinced that long-term investors should maintain a significant position in common stocks.

Today more than ever, we believe that long-term investors should have a meaningful commitment to stocks of well-run companies, companies that successfully reinvest their earnings and generate a rising level of earnings. That is *the fundamental reason for owning common stocks.* Value investing consists of nothing more than purchasing a future stream of earnings at an attractive price. Valuations rise and fall over time, but it is the internal compounding of earnings that creates the secular rise in equity prices and makes them such an attractive long-term holding. Over long periods of time, corporate earnings have risen at about nine percent per year, accounting for the major portion of the total return on equities. Importantly, over the long term, equity returns easily surpass those of other asset categories.

For those who ask when the current economic and market clouds will lift, the answer is unknowable. It may be sooner or it may be later. Take your pick. To debate that question is to risk missing the more important point that the time to buy is when prices are low, which can only occur when the outlook is cloudy. It's counterintuitive, but the environment for investing is better than it has been for years. With many stocks down 20, 40, 60 even 80 percent, the opportunities to invest with the expectation of achieving favorable returns grow daily.

Perhaps the greatest risk that investors face when investing in common stocks is that they become preoccupied with efforts to make short-term calls on the stock market and in so doing dilute the positive impact of long-term stock investing. Those who focus on the long-term and are financially and psychologically able to withstand the volatility of common stocks will continue to be richly rewarded. True ten years ago, true today.

appendix C

Important Information

The discussion of the performance of the Ave Maria Funds (the "Funds") is designed to set forth my views of the market and to provide a discussion of the investment strategies used by the investment adviser in managing each Fund's assets.

Any listing or discussion of specific securities is intended to help the reader understand a Fund's investment strategies and/or factors that may influence a Fund's investment performance, and should not be regarded as a recommendation of any security. I believe there is a reasonable basis for any opinions expressed, although actual results may differ, sometimes significantly so, from those I expect and express herein. Statements referring to future actions or events, such as the future financial performance or ongoing business strategies of the companies in which a Fund invests, are based on the current expectations and projections about future events provided by various sources, including company management. These statements are not guarantees of future performance, and actual events and results may differ materially from those discussed herein.

Any opinions and views expressed related to the prospects of any individual portfolio holdings or grouping thereof or of a Fund itself are "forward looking statements" which may or may not prove to be accurate over the long term when viewed from the perspective of hindsight.

Future results or performance cannot be assured. You should not place undue reliance on forward looking statements, which are effective only as of the date this material is published.

References to securities purchased or held are only as of the date published. Although the Funds' investment adviser focuses on long-term investments, holdings are subject to change.

My comments are influenced by my analysis of information from a wide variety of sources and may contain syntheses, synopses, or excerpts of ideas from written or oral viewpoints provided to me by investment, industry, press and other public sources about various economic, political, central bank, and other suspected influences on investment markets.

Past performance is no indication of future performance. Any performance data quoted represents past performance and the investment return and principal value of an investment in the Funds will fluctuate so that an investor's shares, when redeemed, may be worth more or less than their original cost. Current performance may be higher or lower than performance quoted. Performance data is updated monthly and is available on the Funds' website at www.avemariafunds.com.

An investor should consider the investment objectives, strategies, risks, charges and expenses of each Fund before investing. The prospectus contains this and other important information about the Funds. For a prospectus, please call 1 (866) 283-6274 or visit the Funds' website at www.avemariafunds.com. Read the prospectus carefully before you invest.

Morningstar rated the Ave Maria Growth Fund among 727, 727 and 631 Mid-Cap Growth funds for the overall rating and the 3-year and 5-year periods (as applicable) ending 12/31/2009, respectively. Morningstar Ratings™ are based on risk-adjusted returns. The Overall Morningstar Rating™ is derived from a weighted average of the performance figures associated with a fund's 3-, 5-, and 10-year (if applicable) Morningstar Rating™ metrics.

Morningstar rated the Ave Maria Rising Dividend Fund among 369 Mid-Cap Blend funds for the overall rating and the 3-year periods (as applicable) ending 12/31/2009, respectively. Morningstar Ratings™ are based on risk-adjusted returns. The Overall

Morningstar Rating™ is derived from a weighted average of the performance figures associated with a fund's 3-, 5-, and 10-year (if applicable) Morningstar Rating™ metrics.

For funds with at least a 3-year history, a Morningstar Rating™ is based on a risk-adjusted return measure (including the effects of sales charges, loads, and redemption fees) with emphasis on downward variations and consistent performance. The top 10% of funds in each category receive 5 stars, the next 22.5% 4 stars, the next 35% 3 stars, the next 22.5% 2 stars, and the bottom 10% 1 star. Each share class is counted as a fraction of one fund within this scale and rated separately. Morningstar Rating™ is for the retail share class only; other classes may have different performance characteristics.

Periods ended 12/31/2009	One Year	Three Year	Five Year	Since Inception
Ave Maria Catholic Values Fund (inception date 5-1-01)	37.60%	-5.86%	0.15%	5.25%
Ave Maria Growth Fund (inception date 5-1-03)	26.44%	-1.41%	2.16%	7.98%
Ave Maria Rising Dividend Fund (inception date 5-1-05)	25.29%	-1.29%	N/A	4.17%
Ave Maria Opportunity Fund (inception date 5-1-06)	40.80%	-4.41%	N/A	-1.51%
Ave Maria Bond Fund – Class R (inception date 5-1-03)	10.17%	5.00%	4.46%	4.45%
Ave Maria Bond Fund – Class I (inception date 5-1-03)	10.44%	5.25%	4.74%	4.77%

The performance data quoted represents past performance, which is not a guarantee of future results. Current performance may be lower or higher than the performance data quoted. The investment return and principal value of an investment in a Fund will fluctuate so that an investor's shares, when redeemed, may be worth more or less than their original cost. Fee waivers and/or expense reimbursements by the investment adviser have positively impacted each Fund's performance. Without such waivers and/or reimbursements, performance would have been lower. **An investor should consider the investment objectives, risks, charges and expenses of each Fund carefully before investing. To obtain a prospectus, which contains this and other important information, go to** www.avemariafunds.com **or call toll-free 866-AVE-MARIA (866-283-6274). Please read the prospectus carefully before investing.** *The Funds may not be suitable for all investors.*

	Gross Expense Ratio	Net Expense Ratio
Ave Maria Catholic Values Fund	1.55%	1.51%
Ave Maria Growth Fund	1.60%	1.50%
Ave Maria Rising Dividend Fund	1.16%	1.16%
Ave Maria Opportunity Fund	2.32%	1.28%
Ave Maria Bond Fund – Class R	0.92%	0.71%
Ave Maria Bond Fund – Class I	0.71%	0.41%

Index